**Materialism, Doctrine
and
The Origin of Language**

Materialism, Doctrine and The Origin of Language

VARINDER KHURANA

MOTILAL BANARSIDASS INTERNATIONAL DELHI

Delhi, 2023

© Author
All Rights Reserved

ISBN : 978-81-19394-04-3

Also available at

MOTILAL BANARSIDASS INTERNATIONAL
H. O.- 41 U.A. Bungalow Road, (Back Lane)Jawahar Nagar, Delhi - 110 007
4261 (basement) Lane #3,Ansari Road, Darya Ganj, New Delhi - 110 002
203 Royapettah High Road, Mylapore, Chennai - 600 004
12/1A, 2nd Floor, Bankim Chatterjee Street, Kolkata - 700 073
Stockist : Motilal Books, Ashok Rajpath, Near Kali Mandir, Patna - 800 004

No part of this book may be reproduced in any form or by any electronic or mechanical means including information storage and retrieval systems without permission in writing from the publishers, excepts by a reviewer who may quote brief passages in a review.

Printed in India
MOTILAL BANARSIDASS INTERNATIONAL

To
The Founders
of
Materialism

As a Preface
The Key to Historical Materialism

When the question of the origin of language arises in our minds, it is essential to go to the correct source for correct interpretation. Materialism is omnipotent because it is the interpretation of objective reality. Thus, we have to travel through dialectical and historical materialism; the outlook of Materialism (Dialectical) to reach the destination of truth. Here we want to assert that the present work is nothing in itself, but anelaborated description of the objective reality. We consider Materialism as the foundation for this work, and the founders of Materialism, our sages, and we are just following their bequest.

Here, as a preface, we will discuss an article by Engels; "The Part Played by Labour in the Transition from Ape to Men". This article presents the fundamental consideration for the origin of language.

* * *

This article was written in June of 1876, "...[it] was written as an introduction to his larger work *The Three Basic Forms of Slavery*. He later changed the title of this work to *The Enslavement of the Workers: Introduction*. This was the reason that this brief work touches so many topics; the laws governing the biological and social emergence of mankind, the interaction of society and nature, the possible social consequences of productive activity, the development of the private property, the transitory nature of capitalism, the numerous others" (Andreyev).

But this work could not get completed and he included this article in *'Dialectics of Nature'* by entitling it as*'The Part Played by Labour in the Transition from Ape to Man'*, so it is now a part of the mentioned work. Dialectics of Nature was written in 1883 and got published in 1927; in USSRposthumously (d. 1895). This article also remained unpublished during the lifetime of Engels; it was the journal of German social-democrats in which this article was published in 1896 for the first time.

This Great work of Engels is a firm means to understand the materialist outlook, i.e. the Dialectical Materialism; the outlook of Marxism in real means. This work firmly explains the transformation of man from ape by discussing the part played by labour in this developmental process. Three transformations in apes i.e. the erect movement (walking), the evolution of the hand, and the evolution of the brain, were instrumental in its transformation into humans.

Origin of labour, construction of tools, hunting strategies, and the use of fire were the stages of this evolution as well as the instruments for further development. The origin of language took place as the need of human society, for which the appropriate structure of the human body (which was the outcome of the evolution), played a conducive role. This chapter of human evolution is discussed in the above-mentioned work briefly. The material developed in this work can be traced tremendously in another great work of Engels; 'Family, Private Property and the Origin of the State'.

In the introduction of "The Part Played by Labour in the Transition from Ape to Men"; Engels writes; "Labour is the source of all wealth, the political economists assert"(Engels). But Engels, in addition to this opinion of political economists, writes;

> "And it really is the source – next to nature, which supplies it with the material that it converts into wealth. But it is even infinitely more than this. It is the prime basic condition for all human existence, and this to such an extent that, in a sense, we have to say that labour created man himself" (Engels).

Engels suggested the answer to the biggest question of

history by this sole statement i.e. '*the question of the origin of humans*'. This pamphlet answer that humans are neither the creation of any almighty nor an alien species that evolved differently from the other species on Earth (as it is unscientifically propagated in the name of science, that the humans came or were sent from some alien planets and the other unscientific doctrines of the same kind are also being propagated). Rather, man also evolved through the law of change and development – as all the living beings and matter are bound to change through – from a type of monkeys; called the apes. It is the labour of human hands that created and evolved man superiorly in comparison to other living-world.

Engels presented a strong basis to the fact that living organisms follow the '*Law of the co-relational growth*' and the species which evolved as humans erected their posture to walk with freeing their hands from this function by following this law. He referred to Charles Darwin's *Origin of Species*, "This law states that the specialised forms of separate parts of an organic being are always bound up with certain forms of other parts that apparently have no connection with them" (Engels). He also presented an example from Darwin's work related to this law. It was because of the '*Law of the co-relational growth*', the development of the brain started, and which was triggered by the free hands of the ape and the origin of labour that transformed the ape into man. Engels writes;

> "First, owing to their way of living which meant that the hands had different functions than the feet when climbing, these apes began to lose the habit of using their hands to walk and adopted a more and more erect posture. This was the decisive step in the transition from ape to man" (*ibid*).

According to Engels, the probable period of that ape which transformed into man was the tertiary period and it was "many hundreds of thousands of years ago" and their living place was "a great continent that has now sunk to the bottom of the Indian Ocean". As the initial stream toward the transformation in man had been crossed by our ancestors with the change in diet and the change in the structure and the use of hand as well as feet. But the actual transformation took place with the origin of labour. Before this, they use tools to gather food, to make roofs, for their defence from the predatory animals, but this was not labour in the exact words. About the origin of labour Engels writes;

> "Food became more and more varied, as did also the substances entering the body with it, substances that were the chemical premises for the transition to man. But all that was not yet labour in the proper sense of the word. Labour begins with the making of tools" (*ibid.*).

Early humans, who lived as herds, experienced the profound effect of the development of hands, by the origin of labour humans found a way to dominate nature. Humans kept discovering new qualities of natural things and at the same time, the increased joint activity due to the development of the hand caused social relations to be morefirm. The need to talk within these firm social relations originated the speech.

Karl Marx writes about the origin of language in '*The German Ideology*',

> "Language is as old as consciousness, language is practical consciousness that exists also for other men, and for that reason alone it really exists for me personally as well; language, like consciousness, only arises from the need, the necessity, of intercourse with other men" (Marx and Engels).

Consciousness is a human characteristic. To understand language and consciousness it is essential to keep the following statement in the mind;

> "Consciousness: is the highest stage of material motion (of the dual-fold effect of matter adaptation and reflection). It is a phenomenon of appearance from spiritual and again spiritual from appearance. It is a complex phenomenon of the transformation of the abstract from concrete and then concrete from

the abstract. There is an activity of mind during abstract phenomena and it is human, social activity during concrete phenomena" (Jagrup Singh).

It means consciousness is the characteristic that arises in man because of the social system and it is the higher stage of the characteristics of adaptation and reflection. This characteristic of adaptation and reflection appears as the characteristic of *"spirit"* and *"soul"* in living matter but in man, this characteristic achieves a higher form of *"Mind"* and *"consciousness"*. This consciousness becomes *"language"* in humans, let us see another reference to lustre this concept more,

"Consciousness is the gesture to hold the group together; the voice and the language gesture to attract attention, to the achievement of the human collective activity. It is a complex process of the accumulation of the concrete experiences of practice into abstract concepts and of reproducing them. It gets enriched during the social practice of human development" (Jagrup Singh).

The whole ofthis process now can be understood based on Engels pamphlet, because of the specific way of living of the ancestral man, there must be a gradual but significant different developmenttaken place in the structure of their hand than feet and this differencewas proven conducive for the erect walking posture of man. When they started to walk erectly, they used their hands to gather food which has further been instrumental for the use of tools and ultimately for the making of tools that is known as the *origin of labour*. Here the importance of diet arises and the tendency of migration in animals in the search of new food areas after digesting all the reachable vegetation in one place;*'Predatory Economy'* as it is mentioned in this pamphlet, is an important feature. Different diets from different places enriched with different (and new) chemical features, enhanced new qualitative in body structure. These were the characteristics that differentiated man from the rest of the living world. Our ancestors while living in herds must have been using similar means of communication like other animals. But the speech produced by the human *voicebox* is a human-characteristic. That undoubtedly is the biggest contribution added by the labour in the evolution of man. Speech arises from human social necessity. They had acquired the ability to domesticate animals for the fulfilment of diet, they got meat and milk from their cattle, the harnessing of fire, fire-cooked meat "shortened the digestive process, as it provided the mouth with food already, as it were, half-digested" (Engels, Ape to Men'). The domestication of animals made meat more copious by opening up a new, more regular source of supply in addition to hunting, and moreover provided, in milk and its products, a new article of food at least as valuable as meat in its composition(see *ibid*). These were proven as the strong stairs of human evolution. Which evolved its body, brain and, speech. All these objective circumstances were decisive for the origin of language.

Engels further discussed in this pamphlet; how the idealist outlook originated in human history writes,

> "By the combined functioning of hand, speech organs and brain, not only in each individual but also in society, men became capable of executing more and more complicated operations, and were able to set themselves, and achieve, higher and higher aims. The work of each generation itself became different, more perfect and more diversified. Agriculture was added to hunting and cattle raising; then came spinning, weaving, metalworking, pottery and navigation. Along with trade and industry, art and science finally appeared. Tribes developed into nations and states. Law and politics arose, and with them that fantastic reflection of human things in the human mind – religion. In the face of all these images, which appeared in the first place to be products of the mind and seemed to dominate human societies, the more modest productions of the working hand retreated

into the background, the more so since the mind that planned the labour was able, at a very early stage in the development of society (for example, already in the primitive family), to have the labour that had been planned carried out by other hands than its own. All merit for the swift advance of civilisation was ascribed to the mind, to the development and activity of the brain. Men became accustomed to explain their actions as arising out of thought instead of their needs (which in any case are reflected and perceived in the mind); and so in the course of time there emerged that idealistic world outlook which, especially since the fall of the world of antiquity, has dominated men's minds. It still rules them to such a degree that even the most materialistic natural scientists of the Darwinian school are still unable to form any clear idea of the origin of man, because under this ideological influence they do not recognise the part that has been played therein by labour" (Engels).

Thus, we see that Engels, in a nutshell, attributes human labour as the cause for the origin of science, law, state, and religion and the idealist outlook as well. Due to the lack of understanding of the contribution of human labour in their evolution, many people are unable to understand the exact reasons for the origin of man [and language], and this is why the idealist conceptions are being made anddistorted whole interpretation. Thus, the distorted conception led humans to the distorted interpretation, for instance, as the Idealist interpretation did.

The significance of any work always lies in the overall study of its subject and in bringing all the scientific conclusions to light, that this great work undoubtedly puts forward.

So, this article proves to be an important instrument for the reader to consolidate their understanding of the Historical-Materialism, i.e. outlook of Marxism, This is a great contribution by Engels to Marxism. Which dismantled the unscientific assertion on the origin of man and their language. Engels considered speech as the product of labour instead of any almighty's creation or sudden rewiring etc. Labour first and then speech, these were the two most essential stimuli under the influence of which the brain of the ape gradually changed into that of man, which is larger and more perfect than of the previous. Human practice through senses, especially with the perfectness in hand developed brain more perfectly. The gradual development of the speech is inevitably accompanied by a corresponding refinement of the organ of hearing. So the development of the brain as a whole is accompanied by a refinement of all the senses. Thus, there is no room for any other conception for the origin of language except to consider it as the product of labour.

So we need to ally the findings of linguistics with the fundamentals of philosophy unless we will not be able to get the correct results. Because without the correct philosophical conceptions it is impossible to assert the truth. As Lenin wrote; "Unless, therefore, the problems raised by the recent revolution in natural science are followed, and unless natural scientists are enlisted in the work of a philosophical journal, militant materialism can be neither militant nor materialism" (Lenin, "Militant Materialism"). So to get rid of the pseudo-scientific doctrines for the origin of language, we have to study their philosophical aspects, which we will do in this work; 'Materialism, Doctrine and The Origin of Language' and we have to eliminate all the false considerations.

* * *

Here at this point, we admit, that this might be one of the first attempts of its kind. The limitations in this work are obvious, but we have to present this book along with its limitations. We will try to overcome these limitations in further research and editions. There are huge possibilities of research in this area, especially to going deep into the particulars. This was our effort to address the doctrines of the origin of language based on their philosophical aspects. This work is now presented to all.

CONTENTS

As a Preface		5
I.	**MATERIALISM**	**15-62**
	1. What is Philosophy?	17
	2. Types of Philosophy	28
	3. Idealism	34
	4. Materialism	41
	5. Dialectics	56
II.	**DOCTRINE**	**63-84**
	6. The Formation of Doctrine	65
	7. The Process of Conception, Cognition and Knowledge Development	73
	8. Epistemology	80
III.	**THE ORIGIN OF LANGUAGE**	**85-146**
	9. What is Language?	87
	10. Doctrines On The Origin of Language	96
	11. Philosophical Backgrounds of the Doctrines	115
	12. Idealist Doctrines	129
	13. Materialist Doctrines	134
Afterword		**147**
Bibliography		**151**

Part - I
MATERIALISM

1
What is Philosophy?

Before going into the depth of any field associated with the phenomenon of knowledge, it is always good to start with the morphological meaning of its name, and when we analyze the meaning of the word *philosophy;* we find it as a compound of two Greek words *'philos'* (φίλος, "loving") and *'sophía'* (σοφία, "knowledge") means *'love the knowledge'*.

But the literal meaning of the term never remains sufficient to give the whole explanation, we have to dig deeper to find the nature and form of philosophy. There is a long history of philosophy, but it's hard to find its clear definition; *Why?* Because all the thinkers define philosophy in their historical context. "Philosophy has been many different things to men in different ages. From its recorded birth in the Chinese, Indian and Greek worlds of the sixth century before Christ to the present day it has taken such diverse forms and shapes that men sometimes say there is no one thing that can be called philosophy"(Selsam).This birth of philosophy is being considered in the sixth century BC, and of course, there is no definite subject matter of philosophy as the other fields of knowledge like economics, history or physics, etc. Indeed, it is a broad field and there is a boundless matter in literature and methods are present. The studies and analysis in this field are so remarkably to an extant varied that it is said to have nothing that can be known as philosophy.

"Philosophical problems, however, are called

"eternal" not because they cannot be solved, but because each epoch poses them in its own way. As changes occur in society, life conditions, the volume of scientific knowledge, the degree to which man has mastered nature, and in man himself, relationships between man and the world around him also undergo a change" (Kirilenko and Korshunova).

The phenomenon of eternal change and boundless diversity in the world had always wondered the philosophers and forced them to think about the causes of all these natural events. Humans are noticing the various phenomena of ever-changing nature in the world by acquiring their appearance through their senses since they acquired the ability to memorize and think, the curiosity to know more about the world and its variability aided them to make broad guesses to explain questions such as; *what the world is? Is it changing or not? Can it be cognized or not?*

These questions remained basic questions among the philosophers, and according to the answer they gave to these questions, they can be grouped categorically.

Besides finding the answers to these problems, philosophers also tried to define philosophy as a whole in various ways. Lets us see what, Isaac Newton, by noting the importance of philosophy wrote; "If I have seen further than others, it is by standing upon the shoulders of giants" (Koyré).

This means philosophy leads us to see far beyond our limits. This comment by a well-known person (Newton) in history tells us that philosophy is something that guides us in our lives and no one can escape themselves from philosophy either consciously or unconsciously, but philosophy is like a "giant" which leads us in our life.

Philosophical wisdom mainly has the aim to enlighten the life, lead with foresight, far-sight, and insight and does not only have the task to fulfill intellectual curiosity (Chatterjee and Datta), Almost the same views as asserted by Newton, that philosophy is something which leads us in our life. The phrases like, 'farsight', 'foresight', and 'insight' in later view and 'seen further' in the previous indicates that philosophy is a leading force and responsible for our thoughts and concept-making process.

But a fact, that can not also be ignored is that philosophers among themselves do not agree on the answers of the general questions, and on the subject matter of philosophy too, for instance, there is a line of philosophy in which the origin of life, does not consider as a question, while on the other path this is one of the basic questions, and the same thing happens when an organization *'bans'* the research on the topic of *'origin of language'*, means they do not consider this, even as a question. But we also have many, who consider this question as a basic question of human evolution. *What is happening here? What this trend of opposition means?* The answer to these questions is that it shows *the difference in philosophies.* There is a long series of debates between the philosophers, exists in history, which keeps them apart in their thought. Thought; we consider, the thought of any person, as an outcome of the process of developing intellect, *i.e.* **Thought is always determined by philosophy.**

Then, **is it impossible to define philosophy or its form and nature?**As there are many opinions, those couldn't come to the conclusion for this problem and considered it as a *scandalous* thing and makes an opinion that; 'philosophy is not the 'lodge' for the common people and made it a forbidden type of thing. But, **Does this conception, correspond to the objective reality?**The answer would be a *No,* no; it never reflects the actual reality.Indeed philosophy is not a muddled thing, it is an integral part of life. Yakhot, while addressing the following question of *'How philosophy is related to everyone?'* wrote; "Some of you will be very surprised, perhaps, if I say that throughout your conscious life you are guided by and adhere to a definite philosophy." (Yakhot).

Philosophy is something that guides us, whether it is thinking, or speaking, in making decisions, and presenting doctrines, everywhere philosophy plays the role of determiner.

But it is still too early to give any concrete definition (even at this phase of discussion, its role as a determiner or guide for life is clear) of philosophy, without considering different philosophies in their historical context. Because the objective conditions of society shape the nature of philosophy.

The early philosophical doctrines emerged almost simultaneously in ancient India, Greece, and China, two and half millennia ago was primarily a result of socio-economic conditions of the world at that time (Kirilenko and Korshunova),and it is true for all conditions. If we can analyze and explain any historical development of society, then it is always possible to explain and analyze the philosophy of that time as well, because philosophy is always the product of the historical conditions of any society, and the emergence of thoughts in the brains of individuals co-response to the development of contemporary philosophy. Karl Marx wrote;

> "the thought process itself grows out of conditions, is itself a natural process, thinking that really comprehends must always be the same, and can vary only gradually, according to maturity of development, including the development of the organ by which the thinking is done. Everything else is drivel". (Marx, "Marx to Ludwig Kugelmann In Hanover, July 11, 1868").

As living in a particular society, hundreds and thousands of phenomena come across to a person. While thinking about natural phenomena, human beings always want to solve the 'secrets'. When they tried to find the answers to questions such as from where the stars, planets, and Earth came?, and what is the origin of all things, that exists on Earth? When they are thinking of the question like, what happens after death or what is the meaning of life? They are addressing philosophical problems, either they are conscious of doing so or not, and it is not a matter of curiosity only. Humans face these questions everywhere all the time, whatever the answer would be, but it will always have a definite philosophical meaning.

Till now we came to know that philosophy is an integral part of life, and it is the objective world that is being perceived through practice and generalized by the process of developing cognition at the stage of *'Intellect'*. Philosophy is not rules made by us, but it is our understanding of general laws of nature, it could be limited by the development of social conditions and also by the development of the brain. In its turn, it guides us in our actions and the abstractness enhances generativity, which multiplies existing acquisition and enhances the knowledge base which facilitates practice to create new social conditions.

Philosophy explains the objective conditions as they are, and on the next level, it enables humans to change/manipulate those (objective) conditions. Every idea, which emerges in our brain is the product of philosophy (intellect), originated through several stages of developing cognition and developing knowledge. Marx on the critique of Hegel's conception of Ideal (absolute Idea) said; "…the ideal is nothing else than the material world reflected by the human mind, and translated into forms of thought.".

While discussing the nature of philosophy, Karl Marx in his article 'The Rheinische Zeitung' on July 14, 1842, wrote; "They (philosophers) are products of their time, of their nation"(Marx, "Rheinische Zeitung"). i.e. Philosophies and philosophers both are the product of their time and space; means social conditions are responsible for the origin of philosophies and philosophers. He used an appropriate metaphor here to express his views; "…philosophers do not spring up like mushrooms out of the ground". (Marx, "Rheinische Zeitung"). And further writes; "There is the same spirit responsible in the construction of a philosophical system in the brain of philosophers as the spirit enables the workers to construct the railway with their hands" (Marx, "Rheinische Zeitung"). This spirit is nothing other than of the *'need'*. Human needs are the driving force that facilitates them to set goals and try to achieve them. He then writes about the relation of world and philosophy in the same paragraph as;

> "Philosophy does not exist outside the world, any more than the brain exists outside man because it is not situated in the stomach. But philosophy, of course, exists in the world through the brain before it stands with its feet on the ground, whereas many other spheres of human activity have long had their feet rooted in the ground and pluck with their hands the fruits of the world before they have any inkling that the "head" also belongs to this world, or that this world is the world of the head." (Marx, "Rheinische Zeitung").

Philosophy is an abstract phenomenon. Its existence in the world is through the brain. Philosophy leads man on its path, even if he does not aware of *what philosophy is?*

From the above discussion, we are now able to wind our discussion by framing the form and nature of philosophy in general. By extracting important keynotes from the above discussion we get to know that; Philosophy is a guide to life, that acts as a determiner of our actions, it emerges from the sociological conditions, it is an accumulated cognition/ knowledge base, it is the generalization of human experiences, it is an abstract phenomenon, it gives the interpretations of the objective conditions, deals with the general questions such as the origin of the phenomena like origin of Earth, the universe, life, language, and identify the laws governing these all, helps to change the conditions, and to fulfill the human needs.

So according to this, we can formulate the definition of philosophy as an abstract base of accumulated cognition that emerges from the concrete social conditions by cognizing the generalizations of the results from the experience of human practice. It deals with the general questions of life concerning nature, society, and the laws working beneath as essence, it gives interpretations of the phenomena and facilitates to change the conditions by understanding the essential general laws. It is a guide to life and determines human actions.

Karl Marx rightly said; **"Every true philosophy is the intellectual quintessence of its time"** (Marx, "Rheinische Zeitung"). That winds up the discussion, a 'true philosophy' is above all 'the intellectual quintessence of its time'.

We discussed the form and nature of philosophy so far and found that every human activity is guided by philosophy, whether consciously or unconsciously, *as it is an abstract base of accumulated cognition*. Which always has its roots in the sociological development of its time, and corresponding according to the development of society, the development of the philosophy can be limited. Based on this accumulated cognition, human knowledge about the world gets formulated and human activities take place, which provides new experiences and multiplies existing cognition and knowledge.

When we talk about philosophy and philosophers, both are the product of society, so philosophers are those members of society who deal with the general philosophical problems of their own time by interpreting and explaining the phenomena.

Origin of Philosophy

The origin of philosophy took place after the emergence of the *mind-consciousness,* and *memory-thinking* in humans. The emergence of these phenomena will be discussed in further chapters of this work. At present we will remain focused on the discussion on the stage of philosophy only. *Intellect* is the essence of philosophy and *Idea* is the apparent form of intellect. The actions of our daily life are subconscious phenomena, they have their roots in the conscious actions from which the perception takes place and cognition accumulated.

"Consciousness can never be anything else than conscious existence, and the existence of men is their actual life-process" (Marx and Engels). Human consciousness originates from their actions to fulfill their needs, and memorizing of these actions creates; cognition base in mind, that is abstract, and merely a reflection of the concrete objective reality. Cognition appears as knowledge and this knowledge then determines the emotions, wills, thoughts, and actions of humans.

When we talk about philosophy as a subject, it is a trend to mark its origin from Greek philosopher Thales and aftermath the 7th century B.C.

> "The golden age of philosophy is the three to four centuries after the 7th century B.C. In this period, the creation of the philosophies, from the Upanishads to Bhudha in India and from Thales to Aristotle in Europe had taken place. Both of these philosophical streams by meeting together became the incipience of all philosophies" (Sankrityayan). [translated from Hindi]

The sociological conditions enabled humans to engage themselves with the field of philosophy. Ittested their epistemological knowledge. Thus, the first philosophers arise in the history of mankind. In India, China, and Greece in the sixth century BC, when philosophy appeared to take shape, is the time of the rapid rise in productions and social wealth, due to which a certain section got 'free time' and authorized itself to not to work (that involved physical effort), which gave them time to think and conceptualize their views about the world in general. According to Marx, "The first necessity for philosophical investigation is a bold, free mind". (Marx, "Notes on Epicurean Philosophy - 1839"). The subject matter of philosophy always remains the most general and fundamental laws governing the universe, man and humanity as a single whole; and studies the basis of the unity of man and society, of man and nature (Kirilenko and Korshunova).

When humans started noticing nature, the level of mind and the consciousness came into being, the process of observing (perceiving) a phenomenon, again and again, turns the perception into a notion and again translates a riped notion into a concept, a concept does have the higher degree of abstraction. When a person starts memorizing the phenomena, the loss of its concrete features takes place gently in human consciousness. Then with the experience over time, the accumulation of cognition gained by practice turns into a philosophy, indeed, philosophy is the accumulated cognition base of the objective conditions of the world, in our mind, as they are, indeed. This cognition reflects itself in the form of knowledge and leads humans in the practice to solve the existing problems and to seek new cognition; means the practice of new practice. This process is a spiral shape development, whose every circle is higher and newer from the previous one. Eternal developing cognition of the world in mind helps in the advancement of the development of philosophy. Cognition helps to unite information about the world into a single whole and provides a firm theoretical base, in return.

This spiral development of **Practice – (Cognition – Knowledge) – Practice** is the key to every new thought that arises in the mind and every doctrine is the result of this thought process, the highest stage of the cognition process is *Fantasy,* the apparent form of the fantasy/*doctrine*. Doctrine is always determined by *Intellect,i.e.* Philosophy. and the philosophy itself is **an accumulated cognition base** of the objective world, made up of experience gained through objective practice. "Before there is conscious thought before there is the theory, there is practice" (Selsam).

What is the reason behind marking the 'origin of philosophy' from the 6th century BC? It is why, because before the philosophical interpretations, there were mythological interpretations of the world phenomena. When it was the starting time of the formulation of philosophical problems, the answers were in the form of myths but this narrow bounded frame was started melting. The practice determined by accumulated Cognition and apparent knowledge enabled men to think and understand many phenomena despite considering them as a result of the magic or caused by extra-mundane powers. The causes of falling of rain and hail, and river floods, and other hazards are natural; and there are also materialistic causes behind the emergence of humans and their society, the Earth, and the universe. So they can be explained as natural phenomena, despite being based on magic or created by any super-being. This development of cognition and knowledge through practice enabled man to start understanding natural development and interpret it, rightly. Thinking started overcoming the mythological interpretations of the phenomena of the world, it was the starting of the formulation of fundamental concepts of the philosophy. This happens after the abstraction of experience gained by the practice and enables man to think in general concepts and to look at the natural (materialist) causes of the phenomena rather than any extra-mundane driving force; for change.

As we said earlier; that humans were noticing the natural phenomena, and alwaysremained keen to know the essence (laws acting behind them) of these phenomena. They tried to interpret these laws according to their knowledge. But it is never true to say that they suddenly started noticing and interpreting these phenomena in or after the 7th century and the birth of philosophy happened with the sudden entry of Thales, which means, more or less, humans were living without philosophy before Thales. We know philosophy is an accumulated base of cognition and appears as the knowledge that enhances practice. Thus, it is not possible that before him humans were living without knowledge. No, there was nothing like that, indeed, philosophy is the companion of consciousness; **the guide to human actions.** Then *what was that, that has been marked to start with Thales?* In that period, philosophy came on the record in the written sources. Discoveries of treasures of nature and millions of innovations based on them had been taken out by man epochs before this marked origin of philosophy happened and these all activities were the result of practice and made a great knowledge base for mankind.

In the period at which the birth of philosophy has been marked, the interpretations of the natural phenomena were started, epochs before this period, this interpretation was not so common, and can be rarely seen in the pictorial heritage available in the ancient caves. But as a subject, it got special attention in this period. We have said that this was the time when the surplus production, created the conditions to free a particular section of society from being involved in the production, i.e. obviously 'the aristocrats'. Which, had got enough free time to do so. Before this period (not in sharp measures), knowledge was to fulfill needs but after that, it became a means to fulfill intellectual curiosity for some members of the society.

2
Types of Philosophy

As we said in the previous chapter, every doctrine made to explain any phenomenon is always determined by philosophy and the difference between them (doctrines) is being caused by the difference between philosophies. The difference between philosophies is always caused by their answers to basic general questions as we said, they are; *what the world is? Can it be cognized or not? Is it changing or not?* Engels, framed this as "The great basic question of all philosophy, especially of more recent philosophy, is that concerning the relation of thinking and being" (Engels, "End of Classical German Philosophy").

When we establish a link between Engels's assertion and the basic questions suggested by us, it looks like this; *what the world is? An Idea (Thinking) or Matter (Being)?* He further added;

"The answers which the philosophers gave to this question split them into two great camps. Those who asserted the primacy of spirit to nature and, therefore, in the last instance, assumed world creation in some form or other — and among the philosophers, Hegel, for example, this creation often becomes still more intricate and impossible than in Christianity — comprised the camp of idealism. The others, who regarded nature as primary, belong to the various schools of materialism" (Engels, "End of Classical German Philosophy").

So our question; *what the world is?* Has two mutually exclusive answers according to the above assertion, the essence of the question is nothing other than to note the primacy of the one from the two; Matter or Idea, one from them can be primary, and the other would be secondary to the primary one, this answer makes the philosophers belong to the two different camps; Materialism and Idealism. This difference not only divides the philosophers into the different camps but also to all humans in them because philosophy determines all human actions and actions of all humans. But the actions can vary according to philosophies and this difference is visible in all the doctrines (because of philosophical determination) given by the man to the problems. Even the doctrines are made on the 'origin of language'.

Our next question; *Can it be cognized or not?* There is the same binary of opinions as it is in the answer to the previous one; one view says that the world is cognizable and the other holds that the world is not cognizable. The view, which considers the world is cognizable belongs to that camp, which considers the matter is primary and every human thought is the reflection of matter through mind, and the mind itself gets developed through the process of cognition, as we discussed in the previous chapter. But the people with the other view that does not consider the world cognizable, hold a single view under different words and names that; this world is not real and it is only a reflection of the 'thought or will' of the supreme power, whose 'will' can not be cognized. Let us have a look at what Lenin said;

> "The world is the non-ego created by the ego, said Fichte. The world is Absolute Idea, said Hegel. The world is will, said Schopenhauer. The world is concept and idea, says the immanentist Rehmke. Being is consciousness, says the immanentist Schuppe. The physical is a substitution for the psychical, says Bogdanov. One must be blind not to perceive the identical idealist essence under these various verbal cloaks." (Lenin, *Materialism and, Empirio-Criticism*).

This view belongs to the idealistic camp of philosophy. Who considers the world as a creation of *'ultimate reality, 'absolute idea'* or several other names. But the essence and the central idea of their view are, that *'the world is a creation* in one or another way. So it can not be cognized because the *'will'* of the creator can not be analyzed or understood. So any question or research about its *'Will'* is futile. The same conception was the reason behind the ban enforced by the 'Linguistics society of Paris' in 1866, to discourage the research on the 'Origin of Language'. Because according to them, 'Language' is a 'will' of the creator, for humans.

Our third question was; Is it (the world) changing or not? this question also has several answers but the essence of the answers categorizes them in two views; i.e. 1. It changes or 2. It does not change. This question points, that; Does nature changes its form or not? If the answer is yes, then there are the possibilities to develop new properties, for example, non-speaking humans developed new properties of speech or giraffes developed a long neck or the animals of cold habitat developed thick, dense fur and more. But if nature (world) is not changing then there is no possibility of developing new properties anywhere in nature, because developing new properties means the phenomenon of change. So no change and no new properties shall be developing there.

The view of the changing world is of two types further; 1. Circular change (Metaphysical) and 2. Dialectical Change (Spiral). The metaphysical viewpoint considers the change which has a fixed revolving point and all changing properties revolve in a circle, again and again, to reach the same point and then to again start from that point.

But the dialectical view states that the change happens neither in a circular path nor in a straight line, though in a spiral path, in which every new spiral stage is higher and advanced than the previous one; means new properties are higher and advanced than the old properties. Origin of speech was a new property in a non-speaking human before which humans spent millions of years without speech. But once speech originated, it became a new and advanced property in humans. Since then no human takes another million years to get the ability to speak, and it is being advanced since then. It was a 'change' that happened in society.

Here in this chapter on types of philosophy, we started with three questions. According to the discussion, we arrived at the stage to form the basis on which the types of philosophy can further be discussed. Philosophy on the general questions of being is divided on their primacy basis of either Matter is Primary or Idea is primary. If the matter is primary then it can be cognized and the world is *'matter'*. But if the Idea is primary, the world is the reflection of an absolute idea, which can not be cognized, so the world can also not be cognized. Thus, the binary answers to the first two questions, divide philosophers (indeed humans) into Materialists and Idealists although the answer to the third question (the third question was based on the view that *if nature changes or not?*) Further divides them into the binary of Dialectical and Metaphysical.

Thus, this is the stage to discuss the camps of philosophy, onwards.

Camps of Philosophy

"Earth; the third planet of the solar system has "life", modern stage of the development of life is; human society. Human society is now at its *intellectual heights*. The true philosophy of every society always happens to be the peak of its intellectual heights. Modern Society has the history of the clash between the Philosophy of Materialism and the Philosophy of Idealism." (Jagrup).

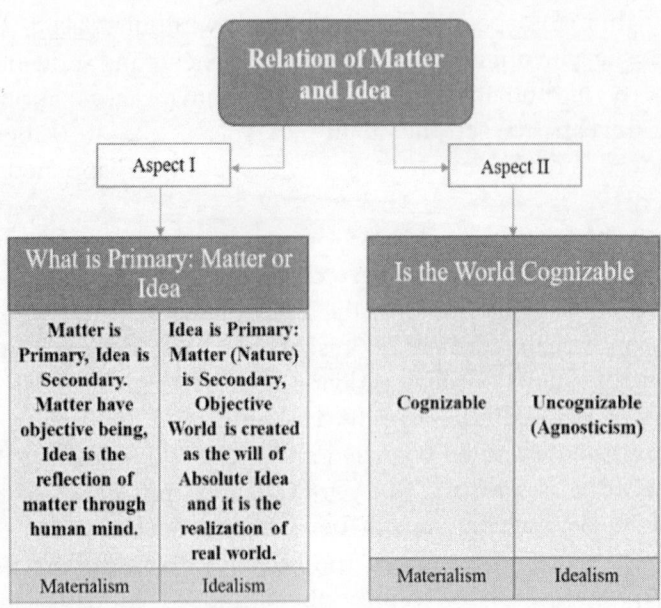

Camps of Philosophy dealing with the general fundamental questions

Camps of philosophy are the realization of the great debate between Idealism and Materialism. This long-gone debate synthesized to many philosophical categories around the world along the time. But they can be categorized based on their essence.

"Nature, matter, is also called being. What connection is there between material and mental phenomena? This is a question that faces us continually. In regard to all the phenomena in the world, we can put it in this way: which is primary, that is to say, which comes first, nature, matter or thought, reason, consciousness? Sometimes this question is put somewhat differently: does mind, consciousness, give rise to nature, matter, or does nature, matter, being, give rise to mind, consciousness. This question is known as the fundamental question of philosophy. Different philosophers answer it in different ways." (Yakhot).

Differently developed philosophies; on the views in which one camp says everything is a creation of a supreme creator and other one says the world is not a creation but eternally changing matter that eternally attains new properties, on these basis philosophies can be divided into two main camps as a whole; i.e.
1. The camp of Idealism and
2. The Camp of Materialism.

We will discuss the types of philosophy in detail but in a general way, separately in further chapters, and will try to figure out, how they deal with the different general problems.

3

Idealism

The answer to the question; Did any 'creator' create the world or has the being existed eternally? The idealistic side of philosophers asserts the world is the creation by a creator; as Hegel said, it is an Absolute Idea; the creator of the world.

> "In Hegel, for example, its affirmation is self-evident: for what we cognise in the real world is precisely its thought content—that which makes the world a gradual realisation of the absolute idea, which absolute idea has existed somewhere from eternity, independent of the world and before the world"(Engels, "*Ludwig Feuerbach*").

Hegel considers an Absolute Idea as the creator of the world, that is not present in the world and it is eternal, the whole world is the reflection of its thought content. As we mentioned earlier, Marx said, Hegel made it (Idea) "the demiurgos (creator) of the real world,and the real world is only the external, phenomenal form of 'the Idea". Accordingly considered that idea as 'Ideal' (the absolute Idea), which does not have any anti-thesis.

Hegel in his book *Science of Logic* said;

> "The absolute idea, as the rational concept that in its reality only rejoins itself, is by virtue of this immediacy of its objective identity, on the one hand, a turning back to life; on the other hand, it has equally

sublated this form of its immediacy and harbors the most extreme opposition within. The concept is not only soul, but free subjective concept that exists for itself and therefore has personality – the practical objective concept that is determined in and for itself and is as person impenetrable, atomic subjectivity – but which is not, just the same, exclusive singularity; it is rather explicitly universality and cognition, and in its other has its own objectivity for its subject matter. All the rest is error, confusion, opinion, striving, arbitrariness, and transitoriness; the absolute idea alone is being, imperishable life, self-knowing truth, and is all truth" (Hegel).

According to Idealism, it is clear as Hegel said, everything in the objective world is error and gloom and only the Absolute Idea in being, which has no oppositions, and everything of the objective world is the realized form of that Absolute Idea. That is the imperishable (eternal) Life, self-knowing truth, and the whole of truth.

The essence of idealism exactly remains the same as mentioned above, but the appearance varies, philosopher to philosopher, era to era. But all of them have the conception of a creator which, they applied to every phenomenon, Even the Language is a created phenomenon according to them.

Plato; the Greek philosopher born in 427 BCE. In the city of Athens, he founded a school of philosophy in 387 BCE, which was known with the name of 'Acadamy' named after the Greek hero Acadamus. Plato's thesis holds the view that every individual idea is universal ... every frame rests in the idealistic world ... our soul was present in an ideal world before our birth ... we can see only shadows of objects because everything is a shadow of the frame present is the idealistic world and we are the shadows of the frames present there in that world.

Russel discussing Plato's doctrine said;

"Plato's philosophy rests on the distinction between reality and appearance ... In the last book of the

Republic, as a preliminary to a condemnation of painters, there is a very clear exposition of the doctrine of ideas or forms" (Russell).

From the discussion on the same page where Russel gave the example of *'cat'* from Plato's *'Republic';* we can understand Plato's consideration of the form as apparent and Idea as reality. He considers that the similarities between all cats are due to the same frame present in the idealistic world whose reflection (shadow) we see as an appearance in this reflected world. The apparent thing is the reflection of the universal frame.

"… the word "cat" means a certain ideal cat, "the cat," created by God, and unique. Particular cats partake of the nature of the cat, but more or less im- perfectly; it is only owing to this imperfection that there can be many of them. The cat is real; particular cats are only apparent" (Russell).

By this doctrine Plato can be considered as a dualist; *Ideal World* and *Material World* are two levels of his dualism. The ideal world is real though the Material world is merely a reflection of the ideal world.

The first level world; the idealistic world is the world where no change occurs and that is unquestionably true and self-evident. But the material world is at the second level in which the change occurs among the things but they are attached to the ideas of the ideal world. They are reflections only. In 'Republic', book no. 6 Plato said,

"This reality, then, that gives their truth to the objects of knowledge and the power of knowing to the knower, you must say is the idea of good, and you must conceive it as being the cause of knowledge, and of truth in so far as known" (Plato).

But about the good (the ideal) he said;

"… the sun not only provides what is seen with the power of being seen, but also with generation, growth, and nourishment although it itself isn't generation."

"Of course."

"Therefore, say that not only being known is present in the things known as a consequence of the good, but also existence and being are in them besides as a result of it, although the good isn't being but is still beyond being, exceeding it in dignity and power" (Plato).

So the idealist camp of philosophy believes, the world is the creation of an extra-mundane power, which they consider as Absolute Idea, Ego, Good, Concept, Consciousness, etc. They have similar views; this world is fake and the real world is somewhere else, *The World of Universals* (Plato), *The Absolute Idea* (Hegel), *The Ego* (Fichte), etc. From where this world is being controlled.

Main forms of Idealism

The camp of Idealism is further divided into two; *'Subjective Idealism'* and *'Objective Idealism'*. Idealism as a whole believes that the Ideal created and determines the material world. But its division in Objective Idealism and Subjective Idealism lays based on the different notions for the Ideal (The Ultimate Idea).

Subjective Idealism and Objective Idealism

Subjective idealism believes that objects are combinations of sensations. There are no objects without subjects.

"For a subjective idealist, the mind or reason is also the foundation of all that exists. But here there is no mention about a heavenly, absolute, divine Reason, for a subjective idealist holds that everything around man is merely a product of his own mind, of his own imagination, i. e., it exists only subjectively. A subjective idealist is convinced that when he awakens in the morning, everything comes into being to disappear again when he goes to sleep"(Vlasova).

This assertion of subjective idealists means that there is no real object in the world, but their existence depends upon the combination of human sensations, which means there are only sensations that determine the existence of the objects, that have their subjects present in the human mind, objects are merely their projection. So these types of thoughts we found as asserted by the Subjective Idealists. But both types of Idealists are essentially meant by the fakeness of the objective world and they consider the real world somewhere else.

As 18th century English philosopher George Berkeley said "To exist means to be perceived."

According to Kant, the world did exist really, that it was not just the fruit of our imagination. But he maintained that we do not know anything about it. We can only speak about our sensations, rather than about what is behind them.

Sophists believed, that only human consciousness exists in reality. A German idealist philosopher of the 19th century, Arthur Schopenhauer wrote, *that the world is our imagination.*

But "One of the French materialist philosophers of the past said that the logic of subjective idealism is that of a piano which has gone mad and thinks that it can play by itself, even if there is nobody to strike its keys. In the same way, a subjective idealist is sure that man thinks, feels, and suffers without any external reason" (Vlasova).

On the other hand, Objective idealists assert that there is a world-mind, world spirit who is the basis of all phenomena. That as a whole means that there is one universal idea that creates and determines everything.

Objective Idealists consider the world "knowable" but they interpret this "knowability", as the man can cognise the world, but not the material world, they can cognize only the world of pure ideas which have created that matter by blowing life into it. According to them, the human soul was once the residence of the kingdom of ideas, so it is easy to "recollect" the world which surrounded it earlier. For objective idealists, the "world" is not reality but a specific, ideal world. Because the human mind was once part of that world, Thus, there is no need to study reality in search of truth, or collect facts, compare, analyze and generalize them, or express doubt. Man only has to think a little-and the keys to the secrets of the universe will be in his hands.

Hegel and Plato are objective idealists. They consider that nature is objectively present but is created by an Ideal. As Hegel asserted objective things are errors and glooms but Absolute Idea (Ideal) is being. Plato said objective things are fake and a reflection of the Universal Idea.

Now the internal difference between them rests in the following phrase that objective idealists at a stage believe that; the created world has its existence although it is the reflection and it is fake but exists and observes change and at some level can be cognized. But the subjective idealists do not consider its existence even. They don't consider the world as cognizable; Engels in '*LudwigFeuerbach and End of Classical German Philosophy*' calls Hume and Kant, the philosophers "who question the possibility of any cognition, or at least of an exhaustive cognition, of the world" (Engels).

Berkeley, Fichte, Hume, Mach are example of subjective idealists while Exetialism, Pragmatism, Neo-Positivism, etc. are examples of subjective idealism. Plato, Thomas, Hegel are among the objective idealists.

Dialectics, which we will discuss in the further chapters is important in the difference between Objective and Subjective idealism. For instance, Hegel was an objective idealist and his idealism was dialectical. Dialectics is a materialist phenomenon, it can only give the correct cognition when it would be applied in its actual form. To wind up our discussion on Idealism, Let's consider the difference between idealist and materialist dialectics in the words of Joseph Stalin and Karl Marx;

> "When describing their dialectical method, Marx and Engels usually refer to Hegel as the philosopher who formulated the main features of dialectics. This,

however, does not mean that the dialectics of Marx and Engels is identical with the dialectics of Hegel. As a matter of fact, Marx and Engels took from the Hegelian dialectics only its "rational kernel," casting aside its Hegelian idealistic shell, and developed dialectics further so as to lend it a modern scientific form" (Stalin)

As Idealist Dialectics is not real because the idea itself is the reflection of the material world. So dialectics can only materialist phenomenon.

"My dialectic method," says Marx, "is not only different from the Hegelian, but is its direct opposite. To Hegel, ... the process of thinking which, under the name of 'the Idea,' he even transforms into an independent subject, is the demiurgos (creator) of the real world, and the real world is only the external, phenomenal form of 'the Idea.' With me, on the contrary, the ideal is nothing else than the material world reflected by the human mind and translated into forms of thought." (Marx, Afterword to the Second German Edition of Volume I of *Capital*.)

So this is our brief take on the philosophy of idealism. We will proceed further to discuss the materialist philosophy in the next chapter.

4
Materialism

It is obvious, that the history of philosophy is the history of the debate between Idealism and Materialism. Here, we are limiting ourselves on the general basis of this debate and tried not to go for the philosophies particulars. Philosophers of the Idealist camp also tried to distort reality by attacking "Matter"; The philosophical category for the things of the objective world. They tried to deny the existence of Matter by their verbal cloaks.

Thephilosophers who belong to the Materialistic camp believe that the world is objective, which exists independently from the human senses and can be cognized and the Idea (& the Ideal of course) is the reflection of the objective world through the mind and translated into thought. "Matter is the philosophical category that denotes the objective reality which is cognizable for man by his sensations while existing independently from them, they are copied photographed and reflected by our sensations" (Lenin, *Materialism and, Empirio-Criticism*).

With the above definition, we find, the objective world, i.e. Matter exists independently, which affects human senses and gets cognized (copied and photographed) by them. This cognization with an increasing degree of abstraction gets reflected through knowledge.

The primacy of matter into consideration consoles the camp of Materialism. The matter is eternally in motion it can never be created and never be destroyed, but undergoes the change in form, from one to another, with the regular quantitative change, it acquires new qualitative properties. Nature is matter and its essence is 'Materialistic-Motion', which is comprised up of its motion in space (change in place) and time (change in form). Nature is eternal for them, no one has created matter, so ultimately nature and the world are not created through eternal and eternally changing. No property of matter and ultimately no human property is the creation of any extra-mundane power. Every new property in humans has been emerging, from the need. "There always has been motion, and there always will be; for there cannot be time without motion" (Russell). Motion is the essence of everything, which determines its being, and time is the essence of change in its form.

As we said in the first chapter that; Philosophies and philosophers, both are the products of their time and space. Social conditions are responsible for the origin of philosophies and philosophers. So it is clear that philosophers and philosophies do also get changed with time and conditions if it doesn't observe changes, then it might be a biased phenomenon. "Materialism did also underwent a series of stages of development. With each epoch-making discovery even in the sphere of natural science, it has to change its form" (Engels, "End of Classical German Philosophy - 1886"). When we come to this statement; "… with each epoch-making discovery … materialism changes its form". Thus, materialists consider, every new development in natural sciences, which changes society and affects its development, affects social-human knowledge, ultimately affects materialism. Because materialism is not a rigid field, that's couldn't experience change. Its development depends on social practice and social knowledge if they change, ultimately they affect materialism, e.g. Materialism was keen to believe that an atom is the tiniest part of the matter, but when physics discovered that atom itself has further parts like neutron, proton, electron, so on and so forth. Thus, Materialism changed its understanding of the tiniest unit of matter, because of the development of human knowledge, development in materialism took place. But the fundamental understanding for the primacy of matter and materialistic motion is constant, remained, and will remain constant.

Human knowledge is a reflection of their understanding of the world. The understanding and cognition of the world depend upon the development of the society and natural sciences of that time, the tools of knowledge, and then, of course, the development of the brain itself. So, Materialism has shown several stages, corresponding to the development of their objective conditions. They are as follows;

Stages of Materialism

- Materialism-Spontaneous (7th – 1st centuries BC), Fan Wanzu, Shen XU, The Charvakas, Heraclitus, Democritus, and others.
- Materialism- Metaphysical (17th – 19th century), Francis Bacon, John Locke, Benedict Spinoza, Julien La Mettrie, Denis Diderot, Claude Helvetius, Ludwig Feuerbach.
- Materialism-Dialectical (19th – 20th centuries), Karl Marx, Frederick Engels, V.I. Lenin.

The stages of Materialism clearly show their development corresponding to the development of the natural sciences. This will never be wrong that the emergence of the different trends of materialism is linked to epoch-making scientific discoveries. When there were no proper pieces of evidence about the formation of the universe, because of the less developed natural sciences. There were guesses about the structure and formation of the universe, early philosophical guesses were spontaneous but materialistic. When there was only the 'Mechanics' developed natural science. The form of materialism was Metaphysical. When the natural sciences had been developed further and came to know the true essence of nature the Materialism-

Dialectical form of materialistic philosophy came forward and is developing so on and so forth. The main stages of materialism can be discussed as follows.

Materialism-Spontaneous

Materialism (spontaneous) was unable to get the right essence of nature, because of the objective development of natural scientific knowledge, the primitive Materialistic philosophers gave the explanations up to that mark, till that they were able to do. They were not able to get the right relationship between matter and mind. But it was their 'need' to understand it, the necessity led them to the road of monism. Monism; All things are explained in terms of a single substance or reality. (Rehman, *A History of Philosophy : 2.1 The Milesian School*). Monism believes everything in the world is being emerged from a single substance. Monist philosophers can be considered primitive materialists.

> "Original spontaneous materialism ... at its beginning quite naturally regards the unity of the infinite diversity of natural phenomena as matter ... and seeks it in something definitely physical, a particular thing, as Thales does in the water" (Engels, *Dialectics of Nature*).

The question, *What world is? Why the world is?* The answer came by negating the mythological interpretation relating to these questions.

Thales; who claimed to be the first philosopher in history asserted all things are made up of water and the Earth is floating on water (Aristotle).

Anaximander said; the primary substance is *Apeiron* of which all the things are made up, *Aperion* is a boundless infinite and indefinite substance.

According to the views of Anaximenes; the primary substance is Air, from which everything is made up, and the world is floating upon the air. He further said Sun and Moon are made up of the same matter as the world made up of and human beings are a micro version of the cosmos.

"Air differs in rarity and density according to the different substances. Rarefied, it becomes fire; condensed, it becomes first wind, then cloud and when condensed still further water, then earth and stones. Everything else is made of these, he too postulated eternal motion, which is indeed the cause of the change" (Diels and Kranz).

Anaximenes did not only considered a material substance, from which all the things are made up. But also asserted that it is motion due to which all the changes between different forms of matter take place.

Heraclitus thought this primary substance is fire; in his view, the noble spirit is made up of fire and bad spirits are made up of water, often spirits are between them. He regards every phenomenon as a unity of contradictions and treats it in terms of self-negation (Bogomolov). The notion of motion is the existence of all things and the unity of opposite by these philosophers laid the stepping stone of the work on dialectics. Even Heraclitus is often crowned as the *'Father of Dialectics'*. And his Penta Rhei; 'Everything flows and change occurs at every movement. Nothing remains the same at the next movement (Rehman, *A History of Philosophy 3.3 Heraclitus*). These notions of change and movement tell that these philosophers don't consider nature a stagnated thing, according to them everything is in motion, and everything changes.

Permanadies was a monist, who believe that everything in the world is one, and considered the eternity of the world; meaning that no one created the universe and it will never be destroyed. He agreed with the earlier philosophers' thought of the unity of opposites, but he considered the opposite of the being and non-being. We can know only being (which has properties) and non-being don't have properties and it cannot be known. He said non-being does not exist. He said nothing can come from nothing. His sage Xenophanes is called the Feuerbach of the ancient world. Feuerbach is the peak of Materialism–Metaphysical. The metaphysical outlook of philosophy considers no change in nature. So when Xenophanes was regarded as the Feuerbach of the ancient world. He must be one of the primitive metaphysical thinkers of his time whose influence can be seen in the Permanadies. According to him, change is an illusion, and multiplicity does not exist, because no change occurs. So everything remains the same and single thing. There is no time, everything is present in one movement.

Melissus does also have the view that objective reality is forever, un-generated, indestructible, indivisible, changeless, and motionless. According to him being is eternal and timeless but time exists. He considers the time infinitive and changing, and passing in intervals. He was also a monist who believe; one is everyone and the same, there is no change, no motion. "He defines being as infinite (Apeiron) both in space and time because it is eternal and immutable and therefore cannot have either beginning or end" (Bogomolov).

"Democritus, who came nearest to a correct view of the world's structure, thought that the single primary base of things were atoms —tiny moving particles" (Kirilenko and Korshunova). According to him, there is a non-changing thing behind the change. He proposed the atomic theory; in which he said that by cutting down one thing, again and again, there will be a point where a thing cannot be cut down into two. Which is uncuttable; the word for uncuttable in Greek is 'Atom'. These atoms are not identical to each other. He also proposed the process of perception based on atoms as; when we see something, its atoms enter our eyes, by this, we can see them. It was almost the right postulation because we can only see an object due to the reflected light coming toward our eyes by that object. To which Democritus called its atoms.

Despite the different outlooks about the motion and the change in the world, all of the above-discussed spontaneous materialistic philosophers agreed on the view that the world is eternal and no one created this world. They asserted that the world is made up of a single material substance, which is the Water for Thales ... Apeiron for Anaximander ... Air for Anaximenes ... Heraclitus said; it is fire. Permanadies also believe that everything in the world is one being. Melissus considered one eternal, uncreated objective reality and Democritus proposed that all things are made up of tiny atoms. All these assertions of one single basic substance carry the view that the world is not the creation of any almighty.

Indian materialistic philosophy of Lokayat (Lokāyata) and Charvak (Cārvāka), denied the existence of any creator, according to them the *Earth, Water, Air, and Fire* are the four basic elements, Life emerges from these four. They said; trying to find the creator of the world is worthless. And there is no heaven, no hell, and there is nothing like the soul which can migrate from the body.

"... man is only a body qualified by consciousness. There is, thus, according to them no Self separate from the body and capable of going to the heavenly world or obtaining release, through which consciousness is in the body; but the body alone is what is conscious, is the Self" (Chattopadhyay).

The question for which their antithesis of materialists emerged as Indian idealism, is the question of *the emergence of consciousness*, for which their view that conscious matter emerges from unconscious matter. Which they were unable to answer properly due to the limited development of science at that time.

"When we look back at these ancient materialists, their understanding of nature of matter cannot but appear as extremely rudimentary. Nor do we expect of them any real knowledge of the central nervous system – particularly of the brain – on the strength of which the modern materialists can argue the same point ... (these were the) ... limitations, under which they are historically obliged to work, they do make a bold theoretical attempt at an explanation of the origin of consciousness from matter, and, among the representatives of the antithesis of Indian idealism, they alone make such an attempt" (Chattopadhyay).

Materialism-Metaphysical

Materialism–Metaphysical, was different from the spontaneous type of materialism, in such a way, that spontaneous materialism did not hold the proper view about the materiality of the world, because their interpretation was merely guess based, but on the other side at the stage of Metaphysical type of interpretation, the natural and social conditions were advanced as compared to that of the stage of spontaneous type.

"The word "metaphysics" literally means "after physics", and has been derived artificially. A librarian in Alexandria, Andronicus of Rhodes (who studied Aristotle's manuscripts), while placing them in order, put the treatises dealing with the sphere of the so-called First Philosophy, or Philosophical Wisdom, after his Physics, a doctrine on nature. From that time on philosophical works as a whole were called metaphysics" (Kirilenko and Korshunova).

But the meaning changed over time. According to Hegel; Metaphysics is a view of motion that is the opposite of dialectics.

"To the metaphysician, things and their mental reflexes, ideas, are isolated, are to be considered one after the other and apart from each other, are objects of investigation fixed, rigid, given once for all. He thinks in absolutely irreconcilable antitheses" (Engels, *Anti-Dühring*).

Thus, the metaphysical materialism is the outlook of repetitive circular motion, that doesn't consider the advance and new developments in the form of matter rather simple recursive changes.

"Metaphysics reduces development to simple displacements, increases or decreases, repetition, or movement in circles, and rejects self-development ... objects and phenomena were not considered in terms of their relationships with other objects and phenomena, but only in isolation" (Kirilenko and Korshunova).

So this view to interpret nature did consider motion; but in a circular path according to them in the material world, nothing new can emerge it did not consider the emergence of new properties due to the co-existence of phenomena and objects with each other.

John Locke the philosopher from the 17th century was of the view that knowledge can be gained only through sensual impressions, according to this view, the mind (this view did not deny the role of the mind in cognition, but it) cannot add anything new to the knowledge. He held the view that at the time of birth our mind happens to be like a *'tabula rasa';* a blank slate.

"At the moment of birth, it contains no ideas and only gradually comes to be filled as external objects act upon the child's sense organs. First, simple ideas emerge (such as sensual impressions of heat, cold, light, darkness, form and outline, motion and rest), and later, more complex ones. However, complex ideas are nothing more than combinations of sensual impressions effected by the mind, so essentially they do not contain anything new. The basic thesis of empiricism as formulated by Locke, is that there is nothing in the intellect which is not contained in sensations"(Kirilenko and Korshunova).

19th Century was the stage of revolution in the field of philosophy, Hegel emerged as the apex peak of Idealism (Dialectical) of that time and hitherto. He applied his dialectical method – on thought and considered it (*'Absolute Idea'*) as the creator of the world – in the wrong direction (upward to downward direction). Hegel faced his antithesis in

Ludwig Feuerbach. Feuerbach was the flag bearer of materialism at that time. He strongly bombarded the idealist nature of Hegelian philosophy. His materialism (Metaphysical) was the peak of materialistic philosophy till his time. While refusing the idealist Hegel; Feuerbach denied his dialectics also, ultimately he asserted that there is no motion in nature, and the phenomenon of abstraction was also ignored, as a reflection of the objective world. He believed in the objectivity of the world and denied its creation but did not consider the reflection of the world through the human mind. By this assertion, he slipped into the category of *Metaphysics*. Which considered motion in a circular way, not in the spiral path (dialectical). This defect did not let him raise himself at a new stage of philosophy.

"The chief defect of all previous materialism—that of Feuerbach included—is that things [Gegenstand], reality, sensuousness are conceived only in the form of the object, or of contemplation, but not as human sensuous activity, practice, not subjectively. Hence it happened that the activeside, in contradistinction to materialism, was set forth by idealism—but only abstractly, since, of course, idealism does not know real, sensuous activity as such. Feuerbach wants sensuous objects, really distinct from conceptual objects, but he does not conceive human activity itself as objective activity. In Das Wesen des Christentums, he therefore regards the theoretical attitude as the only genuinely human attitude, while practice is conceived and defined only in its dirty-Jewish form of appearance. Hence he does not grasp the significance of "revolutionary", of practical-critical, activity." (Marx, "Karl Marx. Theses on Feuerbach - 1845").

Feuerbach's interpretation did not explain the actual epistemological process, he believed that objective reality affects humans, but he was not able to interpret the human practical activity for conceiving the objective reality, ultimately he did not consider the human practice as objective activity. He did not hold the view in which the cognition of the objective world gets converted into abstract knowledge. This knowledge in the process of reflection can be translated as subjects. Which affects the world through human activity. Let us take a few more thesis by Marx on Feuerbach; "The highest point where the contemplative materialism has been reached, is, the materialism which does not comprehend sensuousness as practical activity ..." and "The materialist doctrine concerning the changing of circumstances and upbringing forgets that circumstances are changed by men and that it is essential to educate the educator himself" (Marx, "Karl Marx. Theses on Feuerbach - 1845").

This is how the dialectical nature of the world has been ignored in the metaphysical interpretations. They take it (the world) as a rigid body of material things, that does not have any developmental interconnections between them and no abstraction of phenomenon takes place. They did not perceive the dual concept of *effect* and *reflection*. Philosophers or people with the Metaphysical outlook believed in the primacy of matter and through this, they denied the existence of an ideal and ideal world. But by rigidly denying this, they ignored the dialectical thought process which considers the inter-relational development of matter and idea, and it is *'matter'* whose reflection from mind turns into thought and it is idea reflected by intellect enables us to change the material world. So this paradox of Materialism (metaphysical) was also due to the nature of the prevailing science of that time, *i.e.* *Mechanics;* which considers phenomena one after the other in a circular manner, and lacks the notion of dialectical motion.

Materialism-Dialectical

This demerit of Materialism-Metaphysical gave rise to the new advanced stage of Materialism, i.e. Materialism-Dialectical. This was the third stream of philosophy that arose on board to debate is merely 50 years in Germany. That's why the first half of the 19th century is considered as the time of revolution in the field of philosophy. While philosophy was arising to a new form in which; the primacy of matter retained alike the early materialism but the motion of matter considered as the dialectical motion. Because every philosophy is the product of its objective conditions and this product in return changes these objective conditions. The development in science plays a major role as objective conditions. Science is the discovered objective knowledge (of every aspect) of the related field. It enhances philosophy and the philosophy enhances the possibility for the mining of new knowledge in return. That is why it is a dialectical process whose every new circle is advanced and enlarged.

The conditions which gave rise to the Materialism–Dialectical, are the economic and socio-political conditions, the theoretical conditions, and three great discoveries in the natural sciences. The economic and socio-political conditions were the emergence of a new type of mode of production *i.e.* the capitalist mode of production, in which the philosophical debate between Idealism and Materialism was on the peak to understand the real objective nature of the new mode of production that developed the working forces at the higher level. The theoretical sources of Materialism-Dialectical are the classical German philosophy; Hegel's Idealism and Feuerbach's Materialism. The three great discoveries of the 19th century: *The Discovery of the Cell, The Law of Conservation of The Energy*, and *The Theory of the Evolution*. From these conditions, Materialism-Dialectical arises. The founder of this category of materialism is Karl Marx and Frederick Engels from the 19th century and V.I. Lenin from the late 19th and early 20th centuries. Their philosophy is materialism but the Materialism-Dialectical, Lenin said about Marx's philosophy;

> "The philosophy of Marxism is materialism…But Marx did not stop at eighteenth-century materialism: he developed philosophy to a higher level, he enriched it with the achievements of German classical philosophy, especially of Hegel's system, which in its turn had led to the materialism of Feuerbach. The

main achievement was dialectics, i.e., the doctrine of development in its fullest, deepest and most comprehensive form, the doctrine of the relativity of the human knowledge that provides us with a reflection of eternally developing matter. The latest discoveries of natural science—radium, electrons, the transmutation of elements—have been a remarkable confirmation of Marx's dialectical materialism despite the teachings of the bourgeois philosophers with their "new" reversions to old and decadent idealism. (Lenin, "The Three Sources and Three Component Parts of Marxism").

The philosophy of Marx and Engels was Materialism; as asserted by Lenin. We told earlier that philosophy determines the outlook; through which we see the world and arrive at the particular results as an outcome. This outcome is nothing else than the doctrine. So we came to know that every doctrine is philosophically determined. If the development of philosophy depends upon the development of the conditions then it's obvious that the development of outlook also depends upon the conditions With the advancement in conditions the philosophy and outlook both develop. Thus, the outcome will also be different and advanced. Now, what will be the outlook of the philosophy (Materialism-Dialectical) that considers, *matter eternally changing?* It will the world view of changing matter in its objective conditions; *i.e.* Dialectical Matter, so the outlook will be *Dialectical and Historical Materialism.* Which interprets the phenomenon corresponding to the objective conditions as they are. *New properties emerge from the old properties* will be its outcome (doctrine). This is the essence of *ideology.*

"Marx deepened and developed philosophical materialism to the full, and extended the cognition of nature to include the cognition of human society. His historical materialism was a great achievement in scientific thinking… Just as man's knowledge reflects nature (i.e., developing matter), which exists independently of him, so man's *social knowledge* (i.e., his various views and doctrines—philosophical, religious, political and so forth) reflects the *economic system* of society Marx's philosophy is a consummate philosophical materialism which has provided mankind, and especially the working class, with powerful instruments of knowledge" (Lenin, "The Three Sources and Three Component Parts of Marxism").

These are the stages of materialism along the time and developing conditions. When Materialistic interpretation met the dialectical conception, it became the true interpretation of all phenomena. It is clear fact that when we want to explain any phenomenon we have to track the motion-path of its development. The motion of the matter is dialectical, Thus, the interpreter has to be a dialectical materialist (outlook) to explain nature and its law of development. The knowledge accumulated through the dialectical materialistic outlook enriches philosophy.

"Nothing is eternal but eternally changing, eternally moving matter and the laws according to which it moves and changes...matter remains eternally the same in all its transformations, that none of its attributes can ever be lost" (Engels, *Dialectics of Nature*).

Engels, one of the founders of Materialism-Dialectical, asserts that it is only, the eternally changing matter is eternal and during this change in matter none of its attributes ever be lost, and only the transformations of matter occur because matter can neither be created nor be destroyed, but changes its form ever.

Materialism-Dialectical differs from the prior stages of materialism; it is the conception of changing matter. All the forms of Materialism have no difference in considering the primacy of Matter before Idea. But it is only the Materialism-Dialectical corrects the relation between Matter and Idea, *i.e.* dialectical relationship. That Idea is merely the reflection of the Material World and the production of the Idea is a generative phenomenon, that means after cognition of the material world, due to the characteristic of fantasy, humans can transform the objective world. So, it is never wrong to say that it is human fantasy (imagination) that enables man for discoveries and every new invention. Fantasy is a human faculty that transforms its previous experience and creates new ideas and images, it links up the existent with the probable.

> "Imagination is more important than knowledge. For knowledge is limited, whereas imagination embraces the entire world, stimulating progress, giving birth to evolution. It is, strictly speaking, a real factor in scientific research" (Einstein).

It is the fantasy; that is responsible for the presentation of doctrines. The correctness of this depends upon the degree of true cognition of the world.

5
Dialectics

Dialectics is the science of inter-relation of all matter as eternal relative change; change corresponding to its surroundings. Dialectics is the essence of the eternal interchange of objects and phenomena; Dialectics is the essence of most general laws of development. All the causes of the phenomena of the development of the world can be aggregated into a few basic fundamental laws of development, i.e. laws of dialectics;

> "...from the history of nature and human society that the laws of dialectics are abstracted. For they are nothing but the most general laws of these two stages of historical development, as well as of thought itself. And indeed they can be reduced in the main to three:
>
> The law of the transformation of quantity into quality and vice versa;
>
> The law of the interpénétration of opposites;
>
> The law of the negation of the negation"
>
> (Engels, *Dialectics of Nature*).

How Dialectics is applicable with all things of the universe is an interesting fact, when we are using the phrase, "on all things of the universe"; we are fully aware here that everything in the universe is a form of matter and the remaining, to which we call idea, is the product of dialectics of matter, that emerges from the brain; the highly organized form of matter.

The matter is in eternal motion, and it can never be motion-less, dialectics is the path of materialist motion, due to which relative development in matter takes place. Mater is eternally dialectical. All matter from the tiniest particle to the heavy terrestrial bodies. All the thoughts are dialectical as they are the product of the interconnection of matter and mind, the mind itself is the product of dialectical interconnection of the man with the objective world.

Dialectics is the science deduced from these interconnections of developing matter, to understand its dialectical motion. "The general nature of dialectics to be developed as the science of interconnections, in contrast to metaphysics" (Engels, *Dialectics of Nature*).

Thus, the Materialist-dialectics is a doctrine of the development as the eternal change in nature and society, as well as the instrument to cognize the world... Materialist dialectics has facilitated a correct approach to get the objective knowledge of the world.

Main Stages of Development to Understand Dialectics

According to the development of knowledge of the natural and social phenomenon, the understanding of the essence and general laws (dialectical) of their development also got advanced, and the method of understanding (dialectics) has also undergone development and change.

The stages of development of dialectics are the stages of development of the method of understanding change and development. While motion, its laws, and the phenomenon of change are eternal.

The main stages of the development of dialectics are as follows;

6th – 4th centuries BC, **'Spontaneous Materialist Dialectics'**, e.g. Heraclitus and Aristotle. Engels mentioned this stage as;

"This primitive, naive but intrinsically correct conception of the world is that of ancient Greek philosophy, and was first clearly formulated by Heraclitus: everything is and is not, for everything is fluid, is constantly changing, constantly coming into being and passing away" (Engels, *Socialism: Utopian and Scientific*).

18th – 19th Centuries, **'Idealist Dialectics'**, as of the dialectics of Kant, Fichte, Schelling, and Hegel. Three laws of the Dialectics were proposed by Hegel, but according to Engels, "The mistake lies in the fact that these laws are foisted on nature and history as laws of thought, and not deduced from them" (Engels, *Dialectics of Nature*).

19th – 20th Centuries, **'Scientific Materialist Dialectics'**; Invented by Marx, Engels, and Lenin.

"It is the merit of Marx that, in contrast to the "peevish, arrogant, mediocre, Ἐπίγονοι who now talk large in Germany", he was the first to have brought to the fore again the forgotten dialectical method, its connection with Hegelian dialectics and its distinction from the latter, and at the same time to have applied this method in Capital to the facts of an empirical science, political economy" (Engels, *Anti-Dühring*).

Marx, integrated Materialism with dialectics. Metaphysical materialists while denying the creation hypothesis also ignored dialectics and fell into the deep gulf of mysticism. But the correct understanding of matter is not possible by considering it isolated, Mater and dialectics are inseparable.

"Thus, dialectics reduced itself to the science of the general laws of motion, both of the external world and of human thought — two sets of laws which are identical in substance, but differ in their expression in so far as the human mind can apply them consciously, while in nature and also up to now for the most part in human history" (Engels, *Ludwig Feuerbach*).

Dialectics is the process of development of nature, and society and at the same time it is the method to understand them, both are different and the same, they are one being, two, and two being one. Thus, dialectics can be applied to the process of knowledge to understand it, as it is a human phenomenon, and it is a dialectical process of development. Let us understand the theory of knowledge as a dialectical development. Dialectics; i.e. Materialist Dialectics.

Dialectics as a theory of knowledge

From the previous stages of discussion, we made our understanding of the important role of philosophy in the everyday life, the development of cognition and knowledge is a dialectical process, dialectics is the key of the epistemology; the theory of knowledge. As changes occur in society, its living conditions, the volume of scientific knowledge, the degree to which man has mastered nature, and known about the man himself, relationships between man and the world around him also change. That means the knowledge corresponds with objective conditions. It is the degree of mastery of man on nature. It is the product of the dialectical relations of nature and society. Thus, the aggregation of knowledge; without any doubt is the dialectical process. It emerges from the contact of our senses with our surroundings.

Here we have some other questions, *at which point, the rise of this process of knowledge takes place?* And *what is the degree of the development of the material conditions that are needed to the emergence of the 'knowing beings'?*

The process of developing knowledge reflects the ever-deeper inter-connections of the objective world, it arises at the riped conditions of development in the history of society. Knowledge base initiated to be accumulated after, humans started to perceive the cause and effect conditions of phenomena consciously. Yes, knowledge is the companion of consciousness. Knowledge is at first a social phenomenon and related to the individuals at the secondary level. Consciousness emerges in social conditions.

> "Consciousness is, therefore, from the very beginning a social product, and remains so as long as men exist at all. Consciousness is at first, of course, merely consciousness concerning the immediate sensuous environment and consciousness of the limited connection with other persons and things outside the individual who is growing self-conscious. At the same time it is consciousness of nature, which first confronts men as a completely alien, all-powerful and unassailable force, with which men's relations are purely animal and by which they are overawed like beasts; it is Thus, a purely animal consciousness of

nature (natural religion) precisely because nature is as yet hardly altered by history—on the other hand, it is man's consciousness of the necessity of associating with the individuals around him, the beginning of the consciousness that he is living in society at all. This beginning is as animal as social life itself at this stage." (Marx and Engels).

It is clear now that consciousness is a product of society, and knowledge is the reflection of the developing cognition in humans, consciousness is one of the stages of developing knowledge and it is the reflection of the mind; a stage of developing cognition. The conscious being of man is the reflection of reality conceptualized in the mind. Now the conclusion for this comes out as Lenin wrote three important epistemological conclusions as follows;

1. "Things exist independently of our consciousness, independently of our sensations, outside of us, for it is beyond doubt that alizarin existed in coal tar yesterday and it is equally beyond doubt that yesterday we knew nothing of the existence of this alizarin and received no sensations from it.
2. There is definitely no difference in principle between the phenomenon and the thing-in-itself, and there cannot be any such difference. The only difference is between what is known and what is not yet known. And philosophical inventions of specific boundaries between the one and the other, inventions to the effect that the thing-in-itself is "beyond" phenomena (Kant), or that we can and must fence ourselves off by some philosophical partition from the problem of a

world which in one part or another is still unknown but which exists outside us (Hume)—all this is the sheerest nonsense, Schrulle, crotchet, fantasy.

3. In the theory of knowledge, as in every other sphere of science, we must think dialectically, that is, we must not regard our knowledge as ready-made and unalterable, but must determine how knowledge emerges from ignorance, how incomplete, inexact knowledge becomes more complete and more exact" (Lenin, *Materialism and, Empirio-Criticism*).

As we understood from Lenin's above-given reference is, that things have their existence independent from the human mind, what we have in our mind is merely their reflection which stored in the mind as conceptions (the abstract images of things). These images are created through the human senses dialectically. These images and concept stored in the brain is the knowledge of the world for human. So there is the only sensual perception that falls between known and unknown.

Between this known and unknown, there is the human activity through which concrete sensual perception by transforming in notion and the conception in mind travels to appear as doctrine. Doctrine is the highest stage of the reflection of accumulated knowledge. It is the highest apparent form of the process of developing cognition and knowledge.

Part – II
Doctrine

6

The Formation of Doctrine

We will carry forward from the point where we concluded the previous chapters and discuss the theory of knowledge and the process of the formation of thought; main stages of dialectics in the history of philosophy and dialectics as the theory of knowledge, the process of conception, the process of developing cognition and developing knowledge in this part of work.

The process of developing cognition and knowledge provides a base to fantasy and doctrines. The nature of the process of cognition can affect the nature and truth value of doctrine. At the stage of *Intellect* in developing cognition, philosophy emerges, and the outlook determined by philosophy empowers fantasy and brings forward the outcome; doctrine as its apparent form. Then we would find out the reason; *why the doctrines are always philosophically determined?* Because they differ as being the outcome of different philosophies. Every doctrine is determined by the philosophy of its asserter. Here, we will discuss the formation of doctrine and the role of philosophy in doctrine-making and as we discussed the main camps of philosophy in the previous part. Here, we will find out, how the difference between philosophers, marks the difference in doctrines. Based on this, we will analyze the philosophy of the doctrine of the 'Origin of Language' in the portion of this book.

Our object of discussion will be the process of the

formation of thought. We know there are two views on the cognition of the world. One considers the world can be cognized according to the other one, the world is un-cognizable. Those who consider the world cognizable; accept the proper process of thought formation. Starting from the perception of objective things by human senses through practice. Thus, the abstraction of the objective world in mind through the process of conception is the key point of the process of formation of thought. That, when evolving further develops as *Philosophy (Intellect)* and *Idea* and then *Fantasy* and *Doctrine*. But on the other side; those, who carry the conception for the world as un-cognizable, make many miraculous assertions for the development of knowledge. So the gulf between the philosophies marks the difference here to in the case of the study of knowledge development.

Process of the formation of thought

When human cognition reaches the stage of *Intelect;* i.e a higher stage of development in cognition, Here, the emergence of an Idea takes place simultaneously, Idea is the product of the highly organized matter; it is the product of the brain. Human life is a social form of being, it emerged and has been developing dialectically; its existence is dialectical. Nature itself is the greatest dialectical motion. The essence of nature is Materialistic-Motion. Being of man is a dialectical being. The essence of its development is the dialectical laws of the development of nature and society, they are as follows;

1. "The law of the transformation of quantity into quality and vice versa;
2. The Law of the Unity and Struggle of opposites; and
3. The law of the negation of the negation."

(Engels, *Anti-Dühring*)

Engels suggested these three "Laws of Dialectical Development" during the examination of Hegelianian dialectics, Hegel applied these three laws, on "Idea" and considered it as *"The Creator"* of the whole nature. While commenting on Hegel, Marx said; "To Hegel, ... the process of thinking which, under the name of 'the Idea,' he even transforms into an independent subject, is the demiurgos (creator) of the real world, and the real world is only the external, phenomenal form of 'the Idea.' With me, on the contrary, the ideal is nothing else than the material world reflected by the human mind and translated into forms of thought. (Marx, "Afterword to the Second German Edition").

The three laws mentioned above are laws of the development of matter, then it's obvious that they are also the laws of the development of thought (as it is a product of matter). Engels asserts about the 'unity and conflict of opposition' in the living matter, when he was discussing the polarization of magnets and about the poles of a body carrying an electric charge. He presented the similarity in the basic essence of all life; and in a widened sense, in the basic essence of the matter.

He said; "...in organic life the formation of the cell nucleus is likewise to be regarded as a polarisation of the living protein material".

About the fundamental conflict between heredity and adaptation, he wrote;

> "...the theory of evolution demonstrates how each advance up to the most complicated plant on the one side, and up to man on the other, is effected by the continual conflict between heredity and adaptation."

He considered these two as the 'positive' and 'negative' poles and said;

> "One can conceive of heredity as the positive, conservative side, adaptation as the negative side that continually destroys what has been inherited, but one can just as well take adaptation as the creative, active, positive activity, and heredity as the resisting, passive, negative activity."

He then writes; "But just as in history progress makes its appearance as the negation of the existing state of things,"

(Engels, *Dialectics of Nature*).

As we saw clearly that everything in nature is in dialectical motion, in which there are unity and conflict/struggle between opposites lead them to the quantitative changes, which at a stage – to which Engels called 'Leap' – brings the qualitative change, and this happens by the negation of prior phenomenon, which already was a negating phenomenon of it preceding phenomenon. So this is the whole dialectical process that doesn't only determine the phenomenon and characteristics of things but is itself is the essence of them. Leap can be defined as;

"…at certain definite nodal points, the purely quantitative increase or decrease gives rise to a qualitative leap; for example, in the case of heated or cooled water, where boiling-point and freezing-point are the nodes at which—under normal pressure— the leap to a new state of aggregation takes place, and where consequently quantity is transformed into quality" (Engels, *Anti-Dühring*).

This is how idea emerges in the brain, this is how new properties emerge in nature and society, the ability to speak emerged in mankind exactly by this dialectical process, it was only and only the humans who invented it and developed it to fulfill their need of communication.

The aim here is to discuss the theory of knowledge and the formation of thought, by which we can understand how a doctrine emerges in the human mind. That will help us to examine the truth conditions of the doctrines given on *'The Origin of Language'* in the later part. At this particular stage, we want to clear that, **a doctrine fulfills the truth condition if and only if it interprets the objective reality.**

We are beginning our discussion with a brief talk on the term *Doctrine*. As we consider 'doctrine as an outcome of philosophy'. The emergence of philosophy (intellect) is the most important stage of the epistemological process, which got developed through the stages of spirit, mind, memory and further enabled the phenomenon of fantasy; it is the essence of the stage of Doctrine. What we postulate/propose/ assert/suggest as the probable solution for the given problem is known as our *Doctrine*.

This doctrine when corresponding to the objective reality is known as theory. If philosophy has biased philosophical conceptions *i.e.* do not correspond to the objective real conditions. Then the doctrine can't be true and will never be a theory.

So according to the statement, we can say as a whole that; the Doctrine is always determined by the philosophy of the proponent (the person). The correctness of the doctrine depends upon the correctness of philosophy.

Thus, **"Every true philosophy is the intellectual quintessence of its own time"** (Marx, "Rheinische Zeitung")i.e. Philosophy is the product of the objective conditions and to be true it must correspond to them.

Doctrine is the realization of fantasy *i.e.* the mind generated imagination through the stage of intellect. It is intellectuality that translates the developed cognition and knowledge in the phenomenon of fantasy, of which the realized form becomes the doctrine.

The philosophy, that considers the dialectical development of the world dialectically *i.e.* through the three fundamental laws of dialectics. The Laws of *1. The law of the transformation of quantity into quality and vice versa 2. Unity and Conflict/Struggle of Opposites, 3. The negation of Negation.* Proponents of this thought, believe in the objectivity of the world, and consider every phenomenon that emerges and developed through an **evolutionary+revolutionary** process of aforesaid law of dialectics. They consider, the objective world before humans, as their philosophy is materialism.
According to Lenin;

> "Natural science leaves no room for doubt that its assertion
> that the earth existed prior to man is a truth. This is entirely compatible with the materialist theory of knowledge: the existence of the thing reflected

independent of the reflector (the independence of the external world from the mind) is the fundamental tenet of materialism."(Lenin, *Materialism and, Empirio-Criticism*).

So the truth condition of a doctrine depends upon its correspondence to the objective world. Otherwise, the doctrine will not be true if it would fail in this correspondence.

The emergence of fantasy/doctrine is the result of the developed cognition of the objective world in mind through human practice, as we have been discussed so far. This emerging doctrine enhances practice and can be verified based on this practice.

"... we shall find that the result of our action proves the conformity of our perceptions with the objective nature of the things perceived" (Engels, *Socialism: Utopian and Scientific*).

But on the other side when someone considers the world is created by an extra-mundane power, –this can be said '*the doctrine of creation*" – then every phenomenon in the world can be reduced to the creation by the will of superpower, The absolute power thought and created Earth, once he thought and created human, and finally he gave the language to the humans. He is the only one responsible for all human actions.

The hypothetical *creation-view* is the outlook of idealist philosophy according to thiseverything is created and would be created by that '*Will*', '*Power*', and '*Absolute Idea*'. Thus, this is an Idealist outcome that emerged through the Idealist outlook of the Idealist philosophy. This is the Idealist doctrine.

We have the fundamental question of philosophy as follows, *nature (matter) primary or the thought (idea) is primary?* It is also the fundamental question of the origin of life as; did life emerge through the long-developing (dialectical) process? Or it was been created by some power? this fundamental question is again the fundamental question of the origin of language in the same aspect. Did the language emerge as the characteristic of developing life? Or someone gifted 'Language' to man?

So to examine the doctrines of the origin of language based on this fundamental question we will first go through the various doctrines of the origin of language, before that, we will talk about the Language, in the sense of its nature and use. But the most important task here we have before us is to explain the philosophical basis of the doctrine. So let us carry forward our discussion in this direction as follows.

Doctrine as an Outcome of Philosophy

Doctrine is the outcome of the epistemological process. The transformation of conception into fantasy takes place in the mind, formation of mind happens through the stages of Spirit-Soul. Spirit is the direct base for perception, whose reflection is the soul. At this stage, the concrete and a direct reflection of the objective world as some physical properties of the object act on sense organs as (sensational; color, rigidity, taste, odor, etc.), the collective features of the objects act on the sense organs as perceptional; images of animals, plants, stones, fruits, etc. and the repeating, recalling and reproducing the phenomenon as notion; recalling of the taste, shape, appearance of fruits, stones, animals, etc. take place. The soul is the reflection of all phenomena that take place on the stage of spirit. They are the sensory stages of cognition and knowledge respectively. After that, the logical stages of cognition appear with the emergence of concepts and the formation of the mind. Mind is the store-box where the storage of concepts takes place. The concept is the cognition of the generalized essential features of an object or a phenomenon e.g. Humans, plants, animals, etc. It is an abstract phenomenon. Consciousness is the realization of the mind.

> "...the mind of man generally, as an image of objective reality ... this objective reality reflected by

our consciousness. To the movement of ideas, perceptions, etc., there corresponds the movement of matter outside me" (Lenin, Materialism and, Empirio-Criticism).

Formation of Mind was a phenomenon that separated human cognition from other animals. Stages next to mind take place in Mind; the mind is nothing more than abstract storage of generalized concepts stored as memories. Mind and consciousness are the base for memory and thinking, memory is a must phenomenon for storing the generalized concepts, without which the thinking cannot be realized. The next two stages are Intellect/Idea and Fantasy/Doctrine.

There is a "theory of scientific knowledge" written along with the Doctrine. Doctrine and theory are different from each other in the sense that, the doctrine is that suggested view, which is yet to be proved as corresponding to the objective conditions but the theory is the doctrine that has been proved and is true for objective conditions.

Thus, we aim to show that every doctrine made to explain any phenomenon is always determined by philosophy and the difference between them is being determined by the difference between philosophies. Whose, truth value can be analyzed by examining their relative truth corresponding to the objective reality, by which we can extract the truth and delusion.

7
The Process of Conception, Cognition and Knowledge Development

Sensual perception of any phenomenon is the beginning of the process of cognition. The process of cognition of the world travels from the concrete perception to abstract fantasy, which follows a spiral path of dialectics. "Human knowledge is not (or does not follow) a straight line, but a curve, which endlessly approximates a series of circles, a spiral" (Lenin, "Lenin's Philosophical Notebooks").

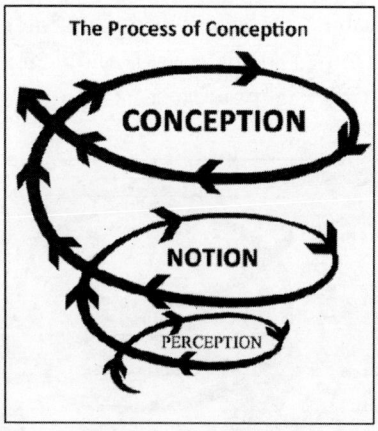

It is the repeated perception, of a phenomenon during the practice, which changes it to a *notion.* When the notion gets its confirmation in the objective world, it becomes a **concept.** This can be recognized as the **process of conception**, At the early time in human evolution, when their ancestors started to use tools, it is an obvious fact that this use would have made their work easier, this must have made their conception to use tools. This process to make work easier and safe, led them from the tool using to be tool-making animals.

In the theory of knowledge, practice plays a driving role. Above mentioned **Process of Conception** is a phenomenon of practice.

The abstract cognition acquired through practice reflects itself in further practice. The phenomenon of reflection (appearance) can be considered **knowledge.** Let's have a look at what Lenin said;

> "…abstractions reflect nature more deeply, truly and completely. From living perception to abstract thought, and from this to practice,—such is the dialectical path of the cognition of truth, of the cognition of objective reality" (Lenin, "Lenin's Philosophical Notebooks").

The practice is a human material activity, which perceives and transforms the objective world and doctrine is a reflection of objective uniformities of the world, a logical generalization of experience and of social practices.

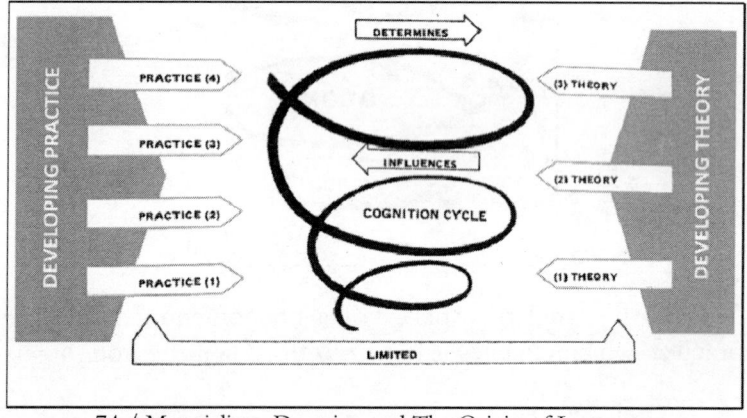

The process of developing cognition and developing knowledge

The emergence of knowledge about any phenomenon and object or even the new inventions are purely determined by social need, for example, the existence of the periodic winds on Earth exist before the human knowledge about them. They came to know about them and their use when there was a need for navigation emerged. When they started noticing them through practice, there was a notion that formed in their mind. They cognized it further by memorizing and acquiring it as a generalized abstract concept, which enabled man to use it in the practice of shipping.

The "Origin of Speech" in humans is also a product to fulfill their needs as same as the above-mentioned example did for him.

Let's now discuss the stages that occurred in the process of developing cognition and knowledge. Whose ultimate product can be known as "*The Doctrine*".

- Stages of Developing Cognition; **1. Spirit, 2. Mind, 3. Memory, 4. Intellect, 5. Fantasy (Imagination).**
- Stages of Developing Knowledge; **1. Soul, 2. Consciousness, 3. Thinking, 4. Idea, 5. Doctrine.**

The above-mentioned categories of stages as **Spiritual** and **Soulular** tools respectively. In the first one, there are stages of *cognition of the objective world* (in the living matter) and the phenomenon of *Adaptation* (in matter generally). While the stages on the other side are the stages of the reflection of the acquired cognition of the world (in the living matter) and the phenomenon of simple reflection (in the matter generally).

> "Spirit (adaptation) and Soul (reflection) are the characteristics of the living matter. Adaptation and Reflection when expressed in the living matter, emerge as Spirit and Soul and the next stages of both categories are the unique human characteristics. Every new stage is qualitatively advanced from the previous one. They appear again and again they have history

and they develop/evolve" (Jagrup).

Both of these stages are related to each other as same as the phoneme and phone (in linguistics) are related with each other; the relation of essence and realization (reflection), the *Spiritual* categories are the essential categories, and the *soulular* categories, they are the apparent or realized categories. The spiritual side begins with the phenomenon of adaptation, i.e. the phenomenon of perception. The process of conception has already been introduced earlier, and the practice of noticing and cognizing enables man to perceive the things and phenomena in the world through human senses, which translates perception into the notion and notion into a concept.

> "…things exist outside us. Our perception and ideas are their images. Verification of these images, differentiation between true and false images, is given by practice" (Lenin, *Materialism and, Empirio-Criticism*).

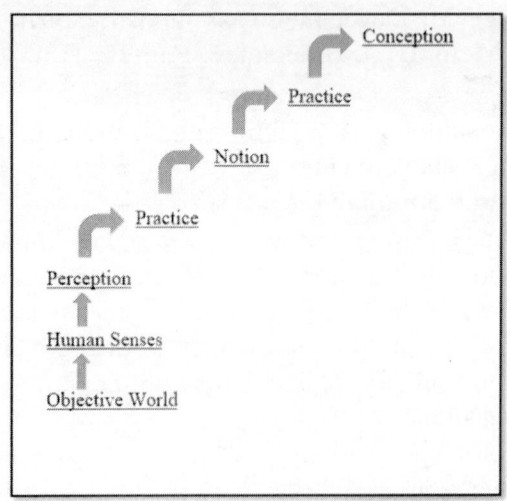

This process of perception is linked with the process of cognition-knowledge development. Perception, notion, and conception are the instruments of cognition. The spiritual side (*Spirit*) is the essence; that is the process of developing cognition. The world is cognizable, and our knowledge is the reflection of the world cognized through the

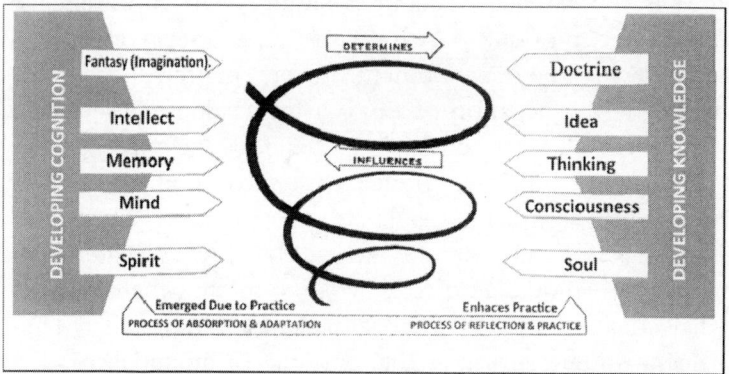

stages of the spiritual side and reflected through the apparent stages of the second (*Soul*) side. The stages of the spiritual category are abstract, but the apparent category side is can be seen reflected in concrete practice. The spiritual stages are the stages of accumulation of the cognition of the objective world through practice and they are being realized in their apparent forms, in the apparent forms of knowledge that determine the new practice and again new practice influences the accumulated (cognized) forms. They change their form with the degree of transformation. As shown in the figure below.

➢ Determination: Objective World Perception (through human practice) → Spirit (adaptation) → Soul (reflection) → Practice
➢ Influencing/Verification: Practice → Soul (Knowledge) → Spirit (Cognition) → Human Practice → Objective World.

Everything in this universe is in motion, it is eternally in two-fold motion, first is its motion in space; i.e. **Matter in Motion,** and the other is its motion within itself; i.e. **Motion of Matter.** The Matter in Motion (**MiM**) is the change in its place, which determines the *Space*, and the Motion of Matter (**MoM**) is the *'change in its form'*, which determines the *Time*.

Space and Time are the philosophical categories, and MiM and MoM (**MiM-MoM**) are their essences respectively. MiM-MoM is the essence of nature. Nature is an appearance of materialistic motion. All things are the various forms of matter, with the development in the matter, new forms emerge by the negation of the old forms due to the eternal quantitative changes, qualitative changes take place as new forms, and all things contradict with surrounding things; i.e. unity and conflict/struggle of opposites. Dialectical-Materialism is the method to study/analyze materialistic motion. To study dialectically evolving matter, there must be a dialectical as well as materialist outlook required. Thus, Dialectical-Materialism is the outlook of materialism, that stands as stated below.

> "Matter without motion is just as inconceivable as motion without matter. Motion is therefore as uncreatable and indestructible as matter itself...Motion is the mode of existence of matter, hence more than a mere property of it. There is no matter without motion, nor could there ever have been. Motion in cosmic space, mechanical motion of smaller masses on a single celestial body, the vibration of molecules as heat, electric tension, magnetic polarisation, chemical decomposition and combination, organic life up to its highest product, thought—at each given moment each individual atom of matter is in one or other of these forms of motion." (Engels, *Anti-Dühring*).

It has been proved scientifically that every object remains in eternal motion and we know "matter can neither be created nor be destroyed" Although it changes its form, from one form to another. The emergence of living matter from non-living matter is the change in the form of matter. Thought is the product of motion as stated above.

We know, various forms of matter absorb and reflect the effect of other forms of nature. The color of any object is the absorption of all remaining colors from the spectrum of white light, except its color, which it reflects. This reflection further affects the eye (another form of matter), by this, the eye can see the colors.

Matter absorbs the effect of surrounding and affects its surroundings. While, in this process, it is eternally in motion; changes its place, and changes its form (time).

This is how we perceive the objective world and our cognition got evolved stage by stage, our cognition determines the phenomena, 'what is known to us and what is not known'. The realized form of the cognized world that appears in our practice is our knowledge and it also got evolved through the above-mentioned stages.

8

Epistemology

Epistemology is the process of the perception of nature in man. It is an advanced form of the process than the process of adaption that takes place in the non-living matter. This process of perception to conception takes place at the stage of spirit and soul (properties of living matter) to the stage of mind and consciousness (properties in humans). The two stages in living matter including humans are called spirit and soul. The process of the absorption of the effect of the surroundings is the ***Spirit*** in living matter. Until the matter can absorb the influence of its surroundings it might seem unchanged, the point (the determination point) from which it moves from one point (movement means reflection) of the form is its ***Soul*** in living matter. Spirit and soul are the dialectical phenomena of adaption and reflection respectively. That means they eternally determine and influence each other. In dialectical development, we know every new circle always has advanced quantitative and qualitative properties. The mind is the processing box of the cognition process where the formation of conception takes place and the consciousness is the realization (reflection) of the mind. The concept is the generalization about any phenomenon or form of thing in mind. It is the mind which appears in the form of consciousness. Next to the mind, there comes the memory which is the essence of thinking; and thinking is the apparent realization (reflection) of the memory. Any concept made by the mind has its storage in memory, e.g. in the concept of the rain, we have a stored memory, that where there is the dark cloud there can be the rain, and we try to save our goods when they appear. Thus, conceptual generalization of the relation of dark clouds with the rain made in the mind is stored in our memory. The act behind the saving process of the goods to save them from being wet is thinking; the reflection of memory. Our tendency to choose the appropriate phonemes in the needed place while we speak a language is the process of memory and thinking. No speech can be generated without the stored memory of the sounds of a language realized through thinking. Humans put them correctly in the right place. This is exactly like the abstract being of a phoneme has their actual realization (reflection) as a phone; the physical sound.

The stages next to memory and thinking are *'Intellect'* and *'Idea'*. *'Memory'* enabled humans to get detailed phenomena stored in mind while thinking enhances practice to get the phenomenon more abstractly, thinking appears as thought. Memory and thinking when reached to a level where it can generalize the essence of things and phenomena, is the stage of Intellect, this is the stage of the developing generalized thought in human beings. The realization (reflection) of memory appears as thinking, this thinking influences and enhances the memory. The accumulation of memory becomes the cause for the emergence of the intellect; intellect is the cognition of the essential laws of the phenomena. The process of getting the essential law behind a phenomenon is the stage where the emergence of an intellectual being takes place. This stage follows the stages of perception, notion, and conception. They cognize principles and set of principles here, next to these three. A principle is a set of concepts of the same kind or the same essence. As "Law is a general, necessary, essential and enduring connection between objects or phenomena" (Vlasova). The cognition of a principle is the cognition of the laws causing a phenomenonand the cognition of a set of principles is to cognize the essence of that phenomenon with all details. The idea is the reflection of intellect, in actual words, it is the realization of intellect, the realized form (an idea) appears when you got to know everything about a thing and phenomenon e.g. in a research problem, you master yourself on every aspect of the study; means when you cognize it completely; at that stage, one would be able to predict and express it's all lengths and breadths.

Until the stage of Intellect, the cognition arrives at that stage where we can consider it as that base of accumulated cognition, which we have discussed earlier in the previous chapters. Intellect is the base made up of accumulated cognition to which we generally call philosophy and its realization (reflection) in Idea is the reflection of the accumulated knowledge of the objective world, and it is the basis of every doctrine which we make about phenomena. Intellect is the full understanding of the phenomenon; understanding all the principles, and Ideas is the realization (reflection) of that understanding.

Here, it is necessary to discuss the property of reflection by matter, reflection is reproducing the cognized objective world in a way and another. Reflection is a determined phenomenon. It is being determined by the objective world and the connection of human sense organs with it. But it is not a necessary condition, that an expressed phenomenon would always be true, there are equal possibilities of the distorted cognition of any phenomenon. Because cognition depends on practice. If cognition of the objective reality corresponds to the real objective conditions, only then it is possible to get the true knowledge of any phenomenon. The practice for cognition can be biased and the reflection; in this case, the expression of biased cognition will be biased. This biased reflection deflects further practice. For example, if we take the question of the origin of language; if we get fail to perceive the real objective causes of the origin of language, our knowledge about the question will remain biased. If the researchers fail to cognize the objective truth properly, their answer will not correspond to the objective reality. Then their doctrine will not be a true doctrine. Let us have a look at the illustration given below; that differentiates the truth and delusion as aforesaid.

True knowledge is the knowledge corresponding to the objective reality while delusion is something that does not correspond to objective reality. This discussion on the truth and delusion was very important to move further because the next stages from both the categories are the highest while we talk about the process of cognition and knowledge development. Because the stage of intellect and idea enables humans to imagine the new phenomenon, it enables them to present your thesis.

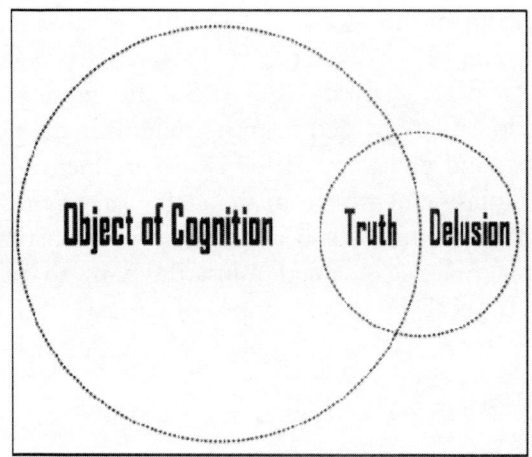

The thesis for the essence of a phenomenon. To present a thesis, it is necessary to get cognize all its fundamental laws as a whole. Then you give your views, whether to explain it or to change it, it will be your fantasy, this is the stage of creative phase of cognition, Lenin said about the fantasy;

"The approach of the (human) mind to a particular thing, the taking of a copy (= a concept) of it is not a simple, immediate act, a dead mirroring, but one which is complex, split into two, zig-zag like, which includes in it the possibility of the flight of fantasy from life; more than that: the possibility of the transformation (moreover, an unnoticeable transformation, of which man is unaware) of the abstract concept, idea, into a fantasy (in letzter Instanz** = God). For even in the simplest generalisation, in the most elementary general idea ("table" in general), there is a certain bit of fantasy" (Lenin, "Lenin's Philosophical Notebooks").

Thus, in the epistemological process, a concept (= Copy of an object) in mind, got transformed into the highest stage of fantasy, this fantasy is an imaginary solution for a problem or phenomenon. When it comes to the realization, it appears as a *Doctrine*, i.e. Every Doctrine is the realization of fantasy. Lenin further noted fantasy on the same page; "...it would be stupid to deny the role of fantasy, even in the strictest science" (Lenin, "Ibid"). So the fantasy is not a phenomenon that emerged from nothing. It is the product of philosophy, and philosophy itself is the product of space and time. So fantasy emerges from the cognition of the objective world in full essence, which is based on previous knowledge and eternal practice enabled mind (human) to present its Doctrine; the realization (reflection) of fantasy.

Part – III
The Origin of Language

9
What is Language?

This part of work contains a discussion on the views related to the origin of language. When we talk about the question of the origin of language, we find a huge number of different doctrines in the fields of linguistics and other social and natural sciences. As we said in the previous discussion that our ancestors have shown curiosity and thirst for knowledge also, tried to answer the question: *how did language originate?* The research related to this question has deep roots. But the early attempts were simply guess-based.

According to Greek historian Herodotus (5th century B. C.); the king of Egypt, Psammetichus isolated two newborn children to find out the oldest language on the Earth, he did so for two years. After the primitive stages of babbling, when they began to speak, the first utterance was the word; *'bekos'*. Bekos; the word for "bread" in Phrygian. Then the king came on the findings, of the antiquity of Phrygian over the Egyptian (Rawlinson). This naïve attempt to determine the ancient race considered the hypothesis of the first native language.

These earlier attempts were not scientific but guesses as we said. Plato in his dialogue *'Cratylus'* while discussing the origin of words addressed the question of the relation of the things and the words; names of things; whether they are natural and necessary, or just the result of human convention. This dialogue between Cratylus and Hermogenes – which

Socrates asked to mediate – is about the *'Correctness of names'*. Where Cratylus holds the view that naming is natural but Hermogenes viewed the naming of things as arbitrary relation of objects and words (Plato and Jowett).

It is believed among the classical Greeks; as expressed in 'Cratylus', a legislator gave the correct names to everything;
> "... not every man is able to give a name, but only a maker of names; and this is the legislator, who of all skilled artisans in the world is the rarest... he only who looks to the name which each thing by nature has, and is able to express the true forms of things in letters and syllables." (Plato and Jowett).

Despite the availability of a large number of doctrines on the origin of language in man, many of these doctrines include traditional and mythological interpretations and some pseudo-scientific factors.

In the previous parts we discussed two outlooks about the formation of the world as a whole; one that believes the world is created and the other that considered the self-evolving eternity of nature. It is not created by anyone. It is the materialistic motion, that appears in different/changing forms, these outlooks are Idealist and Materialist outlooks respectively. Due to the determination of their respective philosophies of Idealism and Materialism, they hold the opposite conceptions; creation versus evolution. Idealists believe in the creation of life, man, and language. But on the other hand, materialists interpret the emergence of everything as developing forms of matter. In this part of the work, we will discuss the doctrines on the *origin of Language* as they are idealistic or materialist in nature. According to which their objectivity will be tested; *i.e.* whether they are scientific or not.

In this chapter, we will start with a brief explanation of the term *Doctrine*. The discussion on the process of the formation of Doctrine in the human mind was the ultimate product of the previous chapter where we discussed the epistemological basis of the formation of the Doctrine and the role of philosophy for the same. In which we came to know that the doctrine is the outcome of philosophy, as that philosophy determines the making of outlook, which results in step by step enabled humans to imagine the solution of the problem facing. Which appears as Doctrine.

In this part, we will analyze some of the doctrines made on the origin of language. Before discussing this, we will discuss Language in the sense of *"What is Language?"* and *"What its use is?"*

Proceeding from this we will discuss the main trends found in the discussion on the doctrines of the origin of language that will play a chain role in our analysis. The intention behind concluding the reviewed doctrines into main trends is our conception that the doctrines are always determined by philosophy, and philosophies can be categorized into two principal trends *i.e.* Materialist and Idealist. Based on this exclusive classification, we can group the doctrines of the origin of language into main trends; that can be analyzed based on their determining philosophies.

Language

Language; either it is verbal or non-verbal is the system of communication among humans. Humans in their social life always need language to communicate with each other, and without language, it is difficult for humans to have a single talk among them. Even it is not possible to name a single thing without language. So language is our social need and there is no language outside society. Language can only be studied properly in the historical context of human society.

"The language gets its existence derived merely from the mutual interactions of humans along with the eternal struggle of the social consciousness and the manifestation of the socio-historical experience created from their dialectical relation. The existence of language is never possible without a social and general socio-historical experience of a community" (Ravinder Singh). *Translated from Punjabi.*

Animals around us also communicate with each other but they cannot do this in the sense in which we usually use the word *Language*. Language as a system of communication is only and only a human phenomenon. It is unique to humans, it is a generative, cultural, and historical phenomenon and in simple words, it is a social phenomenon. Language is a product of human society and can exist only in human society.

> "Production by isolated individuals outside of society— something which might happen as an exception to a civilized man who by accident got into the wilderness and already dynamically possessed within himself the forces of society— is as great an absurdity as the idea of the development of language without individuals living together and talking to one another" (Marx, "CPE")

Thus, language is a social phenomenon, it is a complex system. Many views exist about the origin, form, and nature of language. But it is never easy to define the language system with precision, although not impossible.

According to Saussure "Language is a system of signs in which the only essential thing is the union of meanings and sound-images, and in which both parts of the sign are psychological" (Saussure). For Sapir, "Language is a purely human and non-instinctive method of communicating ideas, emotions, and desires by means of a system of voluntarily produced symbols" (Sapir).

American linguist Bloomfield said that language enabled one person to express a reaction to another's stimuli (Bloomfield). He considered language; a behavioral character like walking, eating, etc. For this approach, this set of behavioral patterns can remain unused for a long period and it can be called into operation by an appropriate stimulus. "A language is a system of arbitrary vocal symbols by means of which **a social group cooperates**" (Bloch and Trager).

According to Chomsky, "...language is a set (finite or infinite) of sentences, each finite in length, and constructed out of a finite set of elements" (Chomsky, *Syntactic Structures*). Language for Robert Hall is "...the institution whereby humans communicate and interact with each other by means of habitually used oral-auditory arbitrary symbols." (Hall).

Language is a system of conventional signals used for communication by a community as a whole. This pattern of conventions involves a system of significant sound units, the inflection, and arrangement of words, and the association of meaning with words (Gimson).

Language is a system of signs for Saussure, a non-instinctive method for Sapir and means of reaction by one person to another's act for Bloomfield, A system for social cooperation through arbitrary vocal symbols for Bloch and Trager. According to Hall, it is a habitual oral-auditory and an arbitrary institution of interaction and communication. Gimson said; it is a system of conventional signals used for communication. For Chomsky; Language is a set of sentences.

We can find one thing common in these definitions except Chomsky; i.e. Language is a means of communication. Everyone seems to agree on this chief function of language; that is communication. But Chomsky's definition of the language quoted above; says nothing about the communication function of language. According to John Lyons, Chomsky Model of Language,

> "It says nothing about the communicative function of either natural or non-natural languages; it says nothing about the symbolic nature of the elements or sequences of them. Its purpose is to focus attention upon the purely structural properties of languages" (Lyons).

In the design features of language Charles F. Hockett mentioned the "Specialization" feature of language mainly as communication, and not to satisfy any other biological function. (Hockett) Humans produce/use language for the purpose to communicate with others. Seven out of his sixteen design features of the language are unique human language characteristics. They are unique to humans and differentiate between language (i.e. Human form of communication) and

Communication in general. These seven design features are; "displacement, productivity, cultural transmission, duality, prevarication, reflexiveness, and learnability" (Hockett).

These unique to man design features of language have a higher degree of abstractness (mental realization of the objective world), this abstractness is led them to a higher and advanced level of productivity. This was something more than mere concrete perceptions, this was the aggregated result of human practice.

> "Division of labour becomes truly such from the moment when a division of material and mental labour appears. From this moment onwards consciousness can really flatter itself that it is something other than consciousness of existing practice, that it really represents something without representing something real; from now on consciousness is in a position to emancipate itself from the world and to proceed to the formation of "pure" theory, theology, philosophy, ethics, etc..." (Marx & Engels).

This is very much understood that language is a system of communication for humans, they created the language to fulfill their social need of communication is a fact that can't be ignored. Almost all of the above definitions ignore this fact and agree only to state that language is used by humans and forget to talk about its emergence. So to find a more comprehensive definition of language we have to move forward from these definitions.

Despite not addressing the question of the emergence of language directly as a whole, ancient Greek philosophers talk about the emergence of meanings of words. They had a view, that words have meaning, either naturally or conventionally.

Both of these different schools have different views on the word-meaning-thing relation. The natural view considered that there must be a natural connection between a word and its meaning because there must be something in the nature of things, on which they can be named. But the other view; the conventional view believed in no connection between word and the thing to which it means. This view states that words attain their meaning due to some people have agreed on this meaning.

Pythagoras and Plato belong to the natural view, i.e. the language had emerged out of the *"inherent necessity"* or *"nature"*. Plato called this necessity; *"spirit"*. While Democritus and Aristotle believed that language had arisen with "convection", and the words are just symbols and no name existed or given by nature. They believed in the arbitrary word-meaning relation. Thus, there is a long debate on the nature of the words, Karl Marx discussed the word-object relation in 'The Capital' as follows;

> "The name of a thing is something distinct from the qualities of that thing. I know nothing of a man, by knowing that his name is Jacob. In the same way with regard to money, every trace of a value-relation disappears in the names pound, dollar, franc, ducat, etc. The confusion caused by attributing a hidden meaning to these cabalistic signs is all the greater, because these money-names express both the values of commodities and, at the same time, aliquot parts of the weight of the metal that is the standard of money. On the other hand, it is absolutely necessary that value, in order that it may be distinguished from the varied bodily forms of commodities, should assume this material and unmeaning, but, at the same time, purely social form" (Marx, "The Capital").

Meanings of the words are the social phenomena, language has the social emergence and existence. Karl Marx wrote in *German Ideology,* about the emergence of language when he called it *"Practical Consciousness"*. "From the start the "spirit" is afflicted with the curse of being "burdened" with matter, which here makes its appearance in the form of agitated layers of air, sounds, in short, of language" (Marx and Engels). So it is the consciousness that causes the emergence of language, not any almighty or any natural inheritance, due to which language emerged. It is the "need" to communicate for which humans themselves created and developed language. This "need" is a dialectical phenomenon, and according to Marx, the need = spirit is cursed by matter (dialectical). It is because of the dialectical development of matter, which cannot be separated.

He further wrote;

> "Language is as old as consciousness, language is practical consciousness that exists also for other men, and for that reason alone it really exists for me personally as well; language, like consciousness, only arises from the need, the necessity, of intercourse with other men." (Marx and Engels)

Marx asserts that "language emerges with consciousness", but he further extends this statement as he said; "(it is) practical consciousness". Means Language is nothing other than consciousness. And it exists in a society for the necessity of interaction, i.e. for the necessity of communication. "Language is the most important means of human intercourse"(Lenin, *Lenin Collected Works Vol. 20*). Here we can connect with the discussion of the emergence of consciousness as described in the prior discussion.

So language is a social phenomenon, it emerged from the social necessity of interaction, and it is practical consciousness. When we discussed the phenomenon of consciousness earlier. We place it under the process of developing knowledge that is the apparent form of mind. The mind is the second stage of the cognitive development process. The first stage is 'spirit', i.e. the need for something, and the mind emerges when the living matter acts for the need, i.e. soul, *'the act'*; the apparent form of the spirit. Which influences the spirit in return and gives emergence to the mind, when the perception turns into the notion. The apparent form of mind is consciousness, i.e. The stage of the emergence of Language. The next stages can emerge only because of language.

Language is not any natural inherited phenomenon but it is a social inheritance. It is an activity of man for cognitive and knowledge development, it occurs as a phenomenon of transfer of experience, gained in the past, to the future generations. Language gives a means of communication to human society as it is its primary function. This mode of communication further develops memory-thinking, intellect-idea, and empowers fantasy-doctrine.

> "The philosophers would only have to dissolve their language into the ordinary language, from which it is abstracted, to recognise it as the distorted language of the actual world, and to realise that neither thoughts nor language in themselves form a realm of their own, that they are only manifestations of actual life..." (Marx and Engels).

To conclude the discussion on defining language; we can say Language is a social need, language is a social phenomenon, humans use language as a means of communication, they interact through language, they transfer their emotions, desires, action through language, they encode them in the symbols created by social agreement. Humans think in language, speak in the language, write in language, and sing in the language, our intellect is in language, our imagination is in language, and our theories are in the language. All these actions are the products of social need. They all emerged from need. They could only appear because of and with the language. The language itself is a social product. It emerges from the social consciousness for the social need of communicational intercourse.

So the language consists of the socially accepted symbols for the conceptions made from the objective world for the concrete things and abstract notions, it emerges to fulfill the social need of communication. Language is a human phenomenon, out of human society (in animals) there can be communication but there is no language. Language is a social product. It is a human invention.

10

Doctrines On The Origin of Language

Discussing language and its development means the discussion of the evolution of language. For which it is necessary to talk about the origin of language. If we would not do the same then we completely ignore the purpose and source of the emergence of language. So without discussing the origin of language, language studies are always incomplete and without knowing the reason and purpose of language emergence i.e. the reason for language origin, we throw ourselves intoa deep mystic gulf.

So the studies on the origin of language are as important as the studies on the origin of life. Those who believe, life and language both are gifted by almighty do not want any study on this topic. As we mentioned earlier the *'Société de Linguistique de Paris'* imposed a ban to discourage any study on the topic of the origin of language (Hewes). This ban was re-imposed in 1873 by the Philological Society of London, its president Alexander Ellis said in his address to the society.

> "We shall do more by tracing the historical growth of one single work-a-day tongue, than by filling wastepaper baskets with reams of paper covered with speculations on the origin of all tongues."

Despite these types of bans, many thinkers have proposed

their doctrine for the problem of the origin of language. Some of them tried to solve this problem correctly, some of them are traditional and mystical, some are pseudo-scientific, whose main motive was never to solve and reduce the mystic elements but to increase the complexity of the problem and to deepen the mysticism and to blur the actual reasons.

To arrive at a conclusion we have to examine these doctrines. Although, the word *'theory'* has been used for all these assertions. But as we discussed earlier; the truth or false condition of doctrine can only be analyzed by its corresponding to the objective reality. Only the objectively proved doctrine can be called a theory. So no doctrine can itself be called a theory without being proved true, based on objective reality.

Those doctrines, in the background, believe that language is the only difference between humans and animals; separate both with the emergence of language, leave the historical development behind the origin of language aside, and knot themselves to the direct and immediate emergence of language in humans; this defines language as a gift of almighty. This view ultimately takes us to the monogenetic view of language origin.

> "...language must have arisen through wholly natural processes, under completely describable environmental conditions, among creatures having less rather than more of the cognitive powers of modern man" (Hewes et al.).

This view conducts the idea that language has a natural origin, i.e. it arose naturally in humans, means without any human effort and humans always had the same cognition powers and knowledge as they have today.

In the *'Book of Genesis*, the first book of the *'Bible'* Old Testaments is all about 'How god created the universe and the Earth and the life on the Earth. God created the first human beings; Adam and Eve. They were created in the image of God (Genesis 1:27-27; *Self Pronouncing Version*). After creating the world and the male and female; God blessed them to rule over every creature in the water, in the sky, and on the ground. God gives the trees to them for their food (Genesis 1:28-30). According to the Book of Genesis, everything is the creation of God, including the man and the female (Adam and Eve). As we discussed in the previous chapter while discussing the types of philosophies; the philosophy whose outlook considers the creation of the world and life is the philosophy of idealism, which does not have any different view on the origin of language too. They believe that language is also a gift by God to mankind. Let's see; In Genesis 2:4-6; it is said that when God created Earth, there was nothing, no shrub, no tree, no rain. Then God created man from the dust and gave him the breath of life (Genesis 2:7). Then God created a garden of Eden for man and gave everything to facilitate him. Even God promised to create a helper suitable for him (Genesis 2:18). Then God enables man to name all the creatures made by him (God). Thus, the man gave the name to all the things around (Genesis 2:19-20). This is how God gifted the language to man. This happened even before the existence of the 'suitable helper'; as promised by God. When the man couldn't find a suitable helper. God caused the man to fall asleep deeply and took one of his ribs and created a woman for the man (Genesis 2:21)

This is how the idealist view in the Bible can be seen to establish, the creation of the world, man, and language. A terminus point was created there on that man suddenly started speaking and naming animals. By this, they establish two things; firstly the world as we see it had not been formed and developed through a long eternal process but was just created in a small period (in a moment) by God for man. Secondly, they separate animals and humans by just one thing, i.e. language; according to this is language the only thing that is special in humans, otherwise, they all are similar creations of God. By this, they tried to blur all the historical causes behind the language origin and establish it as a sudden gift of will. Man and woman; less than twenty-four-hour old were enabled to make large conversations; as they have eaten the forbidden fruit they became intelligent (Genesis 3:1-5). This is how according to the Bible, the man received the gift of language.

The same views have been presented in the Quran; in the 32nd verse of the Surah Al-Baqara (the second chapter of Quran); it is written; "He (lord) taught Adam all the names, then He put the objects of these names before the angels and said; "Tell me the names of these if you are right"(Ali).

According to the traditional Indian view, Brahma is the creator of the world. Language is regarded as the divine gift of God. Bhartṛhari recognized 'Brahma' with 'speech', in *Vakyapadiya*. 'Brahma' is infinite and the eternal essence of speech. Brahma transformed into varied appearances causing the evolution of the world (Madan).

"अनादिनिधनम्ब्रह्मशब्दतत्त्वंयद्अक्षरम्।विवर्त्ततेऽर्थभावेन प्रक्रियाजगतोयतः

(anādinidhanaṃ Brahma śabdatattvaṃ yad akṣaram/ vivartate+arthabhāvena prakriyā jagato yataḥ)" (Bhartrihari).

The gifted beliefs about the origin of language can be also found in Egyptian and Babylonian traditions. According to Egyptian tradition, the god 'Thoth' was the creator of speech. For Babylonians, the language creator was the god Nabu.

The 'created' or 'gifted' view of language origin leads to the monogenesis of language. The view that advocates, there was a single mother language, from which all the languages in the world have been driven. This doctrine is as idealist as the doctrine of 'the first man' and 'the first women'.

"Man fitted to form articulate sounds. God, having designed man for a sociable creature, made him not only with an inclination, and under a necessity to have fellowship with those of his own kind, but furnished him also with language, which was to be the great instrument and common tie of society. Man, therefore, had by nature his organs so fashioned, as to be fit to frame articulate sounds, which we call words. But this was not enough to produce language; for parrots, and several other birds, will be taught to make articulate sounds distinct enough, which yet by no means are capable of language."(Locke).

Thomas Hobbes said, "The first author of speech was God himself, that instructed Adam how to name such creatures as He presented to his sight" (Hobbes).

This type of doctrine we also found when we come to learn about the myth of 'The Tower of Babel' (Genesis 11:9). In Genesis 11:1 of the Old Testaments, it is written as "Now the whole was of one language and, of speech". Children of Noah build this tower whose top was in heaven. Lord did scatter them over the face of the whole earth. This was the day when several languages came into existence with the miraculous intervention by God (Duursma).

This view has the notion that language, separately created at Babel and dispersed into the huge variety of languages as we have them today.

"The assumption of a single original language (Ursprache) (monogenesis of language) presupposes one particular geographical area forming Man's original home" (Berezin). This view establishes one language as a mother language which was the creation of God. So it does not have a single fact that advocates the developmental nature of language. It interprets language as a will not as a need.

Johann Peter Suessmilch in a paper presented in 1756 before Prussian Academy. His view in that work stood on the belief that humans could not have invented language without thought and the thought depends on the prior existence of language. The only way out of this paradox is to presume language as the gift of God to humans. It presumes the pre-existence of fully developed language.

This view of a 'developed language' gift advocates the divine and first language in which the myth of perfection by God stands rigidly. The first language is the language of the almighty. Different traditions assume different languages as this first language. It can be seen as Vedic Sanskrit in India, Hebrew in Jewish tradition, Latin in the catholic tradition, and Arabic in Islamic tradition. Their desire to prove the desired language as the original language can be seen here. The first or original language view ultimately takes us to the monogenesis as we discussed earlier. That is often known as the primitive language.

J.G. Becanus stated that German must be the original language because it is perfect and it had to be spoken by God and by Adam. Noah Webster claimed Chaldee; Aramaic must have been the first language. Joseph Elkins asserted that no language is more perfect than Chinese ... so no language other than Chinese could be the primitive language.

This view of primitive fully developed monogenetic language appears as the view for one universal language. It is the argument that arises with the inquiries in the acquisition of the first language. The question; how humans can speak while other animals can not, and how the languages have many similarities as their structure show few fundamental units upon which their whole system is based? These questions lead to the answer that there was a primitive language from which all languages were developed. In recent times this view can be seen embedded in the universal-grammar view where it is assumed that every speaker has an inbuilt grammar which is common to all languages, based on that a particular language can be acquired.

Some doctrines like "bow-bow", "pooh-pooh", "ding-dong", "yo-he-ho", "la-la" can also be seen around the studies of the origin of language. We can take an idea from the funny names of these doctrines, that they are merely guess-based views. As the "bow-bow" doctrine considers the language originated from the imitation of natural sounds present in the environment and sounds made by animals in particulars, "pooh-pooh" doctrine considers it from the interjection, ding-dong; from the tendency of the natural harmony, this doctrine also consider language ability a gifted phenomenon. "Yo-he-ho" doctrine is based on the work-chant basis, "la-la" doctrine lay in the poetic sources in natural phenomena.

The bow-bow doctrine is based on the belief that language originated through people imitating the sounds of the environment which means language origin has onomatopoetic roots; a dog barks; its bark sounds like "bow-bow" was a source of speech to primitive man. So they referred to the dog as 'bow-bow' nomenclature. According to this view 'primitive man' started using language by imitating sounds of bird songs, animal calls, whistling air, from crackings of rocks, from the voice of rushing water, thunder, Sounds of eating, chirping of insects" (Stross). The name "bow-bow" was coined by Max Müller in *The Theoretical Stage and The Origin Of Language* (Müller).

He (Müller) told in this lecture that the onomatopoeic doctrine was very popular in the eighteenth century, according to which the humans who were mute yet, heard the voices of dogs, cows, birds, or other natural sounds and they tried to imitate these sounds and found these mimic sounds useful as this symbols of the objects which produced them. They followed up this idea and elaborated language.

The main essence of this doctrine lies in the origin of language from words i.e. The naming of the other animals, onomatopoetically. The man continued watching the animals until they found their 'mark of recognization'. When they got that sound by which other animals can be recognized, they named them from that sound. E.g the lamb was named from its bleating sound (Müller cf. Herder).

Another doctrine, the pooh-pooh doctrine has the views consisted at first, the ejaculations of surprise, fear, pleasure, pain, etc. i.e. through making instinctive sounds. According to this, it is supposed that the instinctive human cries, (human; who was yet a speechless animal) or from cries of nature, evoked by certain situations, produced in human hearers certain equally unlearned responses of action based on this vocabulary of familiar sounds making pain, fear, surprise, affection and other sounds like this, the early man started to convey meaning through them (Thorndike).

The 'ding-dong' doctrine held the view about language origin by positing a law of harmony in nature, it means that everything in the world has its inherent sound which can be perceived by us under the appropriate conditions, in much the same way that a bell rings when it is struck. As an object is struck to articulate sound, Thus, man is "struck" when they perceive objects and events in nature, so this is the phenomenon of analogy under natural harmony, according to this doctrine. E.g. "The phenomenon of a falling tree will metaphorically strike the seeing human and will emit the naturally evoked words "the tree falls" (Stross) According to another version of this doctrine, the human is gifted with the ability to somehow perceive the natural and inherent sounds of objects and imitate these sounds Thus, creating words.

The sing-song or the yo-he-ho doctrine postulates that the emergence of language took place from physical environmental needs, the primitive chants accompanying labor. While working together, the physical efforts of people produced communal, rhythmical grunt sounds, which gradually developed into chants, and Thus, as the language. Ludwig Noiré was one of the proponents of this doctrine also assumed that the language arose from the imitation of noises made by the tools at work (Noiré).

According to this doctrine, human speech was originated in productive activity and first arose in the form of abbreviated motions that represented certain work activities and pointing gestures by which humans communicated with one another (Luria).

The la-la doctrine provides the view that language emerged from the romantic side of human life. Thus, it was inspired by playfulness, love, poetic sensibility, and song. The asserters of this doctrine held the view that the need to express love initiated the language in humans. In the book *Language: Its Nature, Development, and Origin*; Otto Jespersen said; "many of the things that fill us with joy in human life ; it inspired many of the first songs, and through them was instrumental in bringing about human language." (Jespersen). This view of language origin advocates emotional over the functional cause of language origin. The language originated from poetic feelings and love play was suggested in this doctrine.

This doctrine about the origin of language suggested that the gesture language is prior to the speech-language, in fact, it suggested the gesture language much older than the speech-language. The list of proponents having this view is very long. They believe that the language in early times was primarily gestural, and was carried on by the hand and arm signals. Hewes in the above-mentioned source said; Nearly all the theories of the origin of language assumes that man's language is, "Nearly all the theories of the origin of language assume that man's language is connected with his superior intelligence and that it depends on more than the presence of organs capable of producing sounds" (Hewes et al.).

According to this doctrine, human speech originated out of the generalized unconscious pantomimic gestures made by using limbs including tongue and lips. These materialistic gestures then become specialized in gestures of the organ of articulation. Because the human hands (and eyes) remained occupied continuously by using tools. The articulation organs' gestures were recognized by hearers because of their ability to reproduce them unconsciously in mind which actual gesture produced this sound (Paget).

Johann Herder in 1769 wrote his essay for the Prussian Academy, in which he noted that language and thought are inseparable, and the human must have the capacity for both by birth.

> "Parents never teach their children language without the children constantly themselves inventing it as well; parents only draw their children's attention to distinctions in things by means of certain verbal signs, and hence they do not, as might be supposed,

substitute for them language for the use of reason, but only facilitate and promote for them the use of reason by means of language" (J. G. Von Herder).

This view advocates that there is no divine source of language origin, as the children themselves discover their ability of speech; language origin in history took place as the discovery of their speaking ability. This ability could not be discovered without reason. The main point of Herder's view is the innateness of language ability. By which he tried to show that humans neither invented language nor it was a gift by almighty but an innate capacity born with them, which they just discovered with reason. It is a part of essential human nature. Thus, he held the views of the monogenetic doctrine of language origin.

Rousseau had the view that language was originated from the "cries of nature" shared with animals. According to him, emotive cries and gestures were used by speechless humans, but they found gestures inefficient for communication, which caused the invention of language by humans out of the cries which were constructed as words (Rousseau).

According to him all of the knowledge is the perception of observable data. He states that the first words were the names of individual things and the first sentences were the one-word sentences. The generalization and abstraction of the names, different parts of speech, and more complex sentences were invented very later. He asserts that humans, 'will to be free' led them to invent language. The languages used by man were crude and primitive according to him. Rousseau was not in the favor of divine origin of language as he held the view that languages are human inventions.

Philip Lieberman has the evolutionary view of language origin. According to him, "... humans have been developed special modifications in their vocal tract to produce speech. He compared the ability to produce speech with ability use tools, as the latter depends, in part, on having an opposable thumb and an erect posture, the former depends upon having a mouth, tongue, larynx, and pharynx, which are adapted towards speech production. He asserts that speech production is not an overlaid function, that uses the mechanism evolved for other functions, *i.e.* eating and breathing. But it was especially evolved for the production of speech" (Lieberman, "Primate Vocalizations").

According to him the acquisition of language probably took place abruptly when the number of calls and cries could be made with the available vocal mechanism (at that time) increased till that point where it was more efficient to code features. He differentiates the primitive cries and the language where the former had the fixed sound-meaning but the latter has the abstraction in the meaning which is not destitute on sound.

No person would dispute that human beings have an innate capacity to acquire language. It is clear that neurologically intact infants and children raised under "normal" circumstances have the biological capacity to learn any language." (Lieberman, "Neural Bases of Human Language").

According to Lieberman; Speech production and speech perception matching are necessary according to Liebermann *i.e.* output mechanism and central mental ability. Both of these may have developed together. By stating this view, he advocates the universal grammar and innate ability for language.

Speech is so essential for the concepts of intelligence that its possession is virtually related to humans. Human is the animals who talk, what differentiates humans apart from other animals is the "gift" of speech (Lieberman, *Eve Spoke*). Bigger brain resulted from more meat-eating led to the premature birth of humans, erect stance altered the shape of the mouth and vocal tract allowing a range of coherent sounds to be uttered (Aitchison).

According to McCrone; Language started with an ape that learned to speak. Ancestors of humans had solved the key problems, such as how to find enough food to feed their rather oversized brains. So when our ancestors happened on the trick of language with which new mental landscape opened suddenly. Humans became self-aware and self-possessed (McCrone).

Michel Corballis held the view that language developed gradually instead of rapidly as it did not start with an ape who learned to speak rapidly. He stated that this gradual process started with the gesture of apes and due to the evolution of bipedal hominids, it got momentum. The large brain that appeared in genus *Homo,* about two million years ago, might have signaled and developed later the syntax and vocalization. According to him the distinguishing point to *Homo sapiens* was the final switch to the autonomous vocal language from the mixture of gestural+vocal system. The new vocal language was supplemented by the gestures but was no longer dependent on it (Corballis, *From Hand to Mouth*). He distinguishes man from other animals in the terms of language.

Chomsky regards the "Language faculty" as an organ of the body, it is one of the components of the intellectual and moral nature of humans; the capacities of humans for creative imagination, mathematics, language, interpretation, and recording of natural phenomena, capacities for complex social practices, according to him; "...a complex of capacities that seem to have crystallized fairly recently, perhaps a little over 50,000 years ago, among a small breeding group of which we are all descendants—a complex that sets humans apart rather sharply from other animals, including other hominids, judging by traces they have left in the archaeological record. The nature of the "human capacity," as some researchers now call it, remains a considerable mystery. It was one element of a famous disagreement between the two founders of the theory of evolution, with Wallace holding, contrary to Darwin, that evolution of these faculties cannot be accounted for in terms of variation and natural selection alone, but requires "some other influence, law, or agency," some principle of nature alongside gravitation, cohesion, and other forces without which the material universe could not exist" (Chomsky, "Three Factors").

Chomsky considers language, depends on a biologically determined instinct, which he called *"Universal Grammar"* and the studies of language evolution are specifically concerned with UG and its origins (see Chomsky, "Evo Devo Theses"). The origin of language is the origin of innate universal grammar for Chomsky.

Human language faculty is essential for their intellectual capacity according to him. Chomsky believes that language invention is "sudden and emergent", that became "releasing stimulus" for the appearance of human capacity. This sudden "genetic event" that rewired the brain, originated the language with rich syntax, that provides a multitude of modes of expression of thought, a prerequisite for social development, and sharp changes of behavior. Chomsky states that this decisive event (emergence of language; unique and sudden) occurred at a point of time after our species itself emerged, but before the migration of our ancestors out from Africa to eventually populate the globe. The time is "Roughly 100,000+ years ago," Chomsky writes, "the first question [why there are languages at all?] did not arise because there were no languages" (see Chomsky, "Evo Devo Theses"). This immediately built ability of language is *"Internal-Language"* (the *"I-Language"*) according to him. The languages we actually speak or sign are secondary to I-language and are sometimes referred to as external languages, or E-language Thus, *"External-Language"* (the *E-Language)* fulfills the function of communication. Chomsky said the *"rewiring"* in the brain took place in an individual (called him *Prometheus*) within the small group from which we are all descended. But this rewiring was uncertain according to him; "Perhaps it was an automatic consequence of absolute brain size, as Striedter suggests, or perhaps some minor chance mutation" (Chomsky, "Biolinguistic Explorations").

Let us have a look at another "popular" intelligentsia

considering the accidental mutation aka sudden rewiring of the brain; "The most commonly believed theory argues that accidental genetic mutations changed the inner wiring of the brains of Sapiens, enabling them to think in unprecedented ways and to communicate using an altogether new type of language" (Harari). This consideration is against the scientific evolutionary process and follows the Chomskyian line; they ignore " ... they creative human impulse and socio-economic needs play a key role in the use of language"(Ejaz). Chomsky opposed the evolution of language through natural selection. He holds the view that "...language cannot have evolved through natural selection because the internal symbols of I-language have no reference to the external world and so could not have been "selected" (Corballis, *The Truth about Language*). Chomsky does not believe in the relation of words and the entities of the objective world. "even the simplest words and concepts of human language and thought lack the relation to mind-independent entities" (Chomsky, "Evo Devo Theses"). This is the case to accept only the abstract conception and of denying its relation to objective entities in the name of *"arbitrariness"*. It distorts the process of abstraction. Chomsky believes that experience can't shape language.

By this Chomsky applies his nativism according to which the human mind has an inbuilt capacity of language, and it cannot be learned with experience, so the human mind has a special component to which he termed as language faculty, that other species do not have.

This assertion leads to the notion of the sudden emergence of language faculty, by which it is assumed that one single event in the history of mankind enabled them to acquire language. But the cause behind the origin of the language faculty is not mentioned by Chomsky.

According to Skinner language can be described in the context of animal behavior, this behaviorist understanding doesn't see any special discontinuity between man and other animals. He explained language in the sense of basic behavioral principles derived from working with animals, principally pigeons. According to his work *'Verbal Behavior*' (1957); language should not be identified with speech but is rather a form of behavior.

Whereas Charles Darwin did not consider language as an instinct phenomenon. Because humans have to learn the language, they have an instinctive tendency to learn the language; the language they are exposed to. He denied the *doctrine of the creation of language;* as

"I conclude that the extremely complex and regular construction of many barbarous languages, is no proof that they owe their origin to a special act of creation. Nor, as we have seen, does the faculty of articulate speech in itself offer any insuperable objection to the belief that man has been developed from some lower form." (Darwin). This is how he didn't only deny the creationist doctrine, but also advocated the evolution of man and its language.

Let's see what Pavlov said;

"When the developing animal world reached the stage of man, an extremely important addition was made to the mechanisms of the nervous activity. In the animal, reality is signalized almost exclusively by stimulations and by the traces they leave in the cerebral hemispheres, which come directly to the special cells of the visual auditory or other receptors of the organism. This is what we, too, possess as impressions, sensations and notions of the world around us, both the natural and the social — with the exception of the words heard or seen. This is the first system of signals of reality common to man and animals. But speech constitutes a second signalling system of reality which is peculiarly ours, being the signal of the first signals. On the one hand, numerous speech stimulations have removed us from reality, and we must always remember this in order not to distort our attitude to reality. Oh the other hand, it is precisely speech which has made us human, a subject

> on which I need not dwell in detail here. However, it cannot be doubted that the fundamental laws governing the activity of the first signalling system must also govern that of the second, because it, too, is activity of the same nervous tissue" (Pavlov).

According to this statement by Pavlov, we can extract the difference between the first and second signaling systems, it is the abstraction; that starts from the sensations and arrives at conceptions, traveling through perception and notion, that is governed by the laws of dialectics.

> "…[Pavlov's] theoretical generalizations revealed the nature of the higher nervous activity and led him to the concept of the first and second signalling systems, of which he regarded the latter as peculiar to the human brain" (Berezin).

Language; the uniqueness of humans among other animals, has the roots in that uniqueness that made man. The appearance of *'Labor'* marked the emergence of the *'tool-making'* animal; who could only use the tools till then; discovered the ability to make them; this was the emergence of the phenomenon of labor. It initiated the eternal phenomenon of the development of tools and the phenomenon of the own development of man. Thus, humans on one side developed tools and themselves on the other.

> "It was labour alone that created a new element, the appearance of which marked the birth of fully-fledged man, namely, society. And language, a doubly important medium having a close relationship to thinking and an essential social function, makes man human and fundamentally distinguishes him from the animals" (Berezin).

Language is a social phenomenon and it is labour that created man and their society, Thus, we saw in the opposition of the doctrines of the divine origin of life, humans, and language that believe, God is the creator of all, there is another view; that asserts; labor is the creator of man.

> "First labour, after it and then with it speech—these

were the two most essential stimuli under the influence of which the brain of the ape gradually changed into that of man" (Engels, *Transition from Ape to Man*).

According to Engels; the development of the brain affected the labor processes, and social intercourse Thus, developed a greater capacity for language, reflection, judgment, and abstract thought. The effects accumulated from these results of the interacting processes led the human evolution.

The combination of hands, speech organs, and the brain made them capable to execute more complicated activities. More complications in activities required more the application of the brain for them to discover new ways to fulfill them. With more discoveries and enhanced use of the brain to solve complex problems, more accumulation of experience took place. Accumulation of experience enhanced the knowledge and developed the brain more. This social accumulation of knowledge, skill, and expertise with its intergeneration transfer (from present to next-generation) ensured the cultural evolution.

"...the development of labour necessarily helped to bring the members of society closer together by increasing cases of mutual support and joint activity, and by making clear the advantage of this joint activity to each individual. In short, men in the making arrived at the point where they had something to say to each other. Necessity created the organ; the undeveloped larynx of the ape was slowly but surely transformed by modulation to produce constantly more developed modulation, and the organs of the mouth gradually learned to pronounce one articulate sound after another. Comparison with animals proves that this explanation of the origin of language from and in the process of labour is the only correct one" (Engels, *Transition from Ape to Man*).

The process of tool-making and social labor always and must need development in the *"thought process"* simultaneously. The faculty of mental abstractness must have to be developed by humans as the advanced result of their evolution. Marx wrote the following lines exactly for this case while comparing the operations performed by spiders and bees with the skills of a weaver and an architect in building their net and cell respectively with the human function resembling these. He said about the distinguishing element;

> "...what distinguishes the worst architect from the best of bees is that the architect builds the cell in his mind before he constructs it in wax"(Marx, *Cap. A Crit. Polit. Econ.*).

The human ability to translateconcrete in the abstract; the capacity to create a mental picture of a situation by developing the abstract conception of the immediate surroundings in the mind. This ability of abstractness led the ancestors to be humans. The step that was taken for the production of the tool was purely urged by the necessity; the necessity to fulfill the purpose to make the practice easy. Tools that could make this process easy on one hand, and enhance the quantity of the production on the other. The easy availability of enough diet made those circumstances for the body that developed the human body and brain more rapidly than ever before; according to the materialist doctrine. Accordingly, language in humans originated from the necessity of interaction between them in society. The development of erect human posture made the hands free to be used to handle tools first and then for making tools. Due to erect posture; the reshaping of the sound organs took place. Though the development of the human brain enhanced the process of abstract conceptions. These relative circumstances made language emerge in humans and humans only.

The biggest condition for the emergence of language in human society. The chief function of language is communication and language is *"practical consciousness"* for Marx, he said;

> "Language is as old as consciousness, language is

practical, real consciousness that exists for other men as well, and only therefore does it also exist for me; language, like consciousness, only arises from the need, the necessity, of intercourse with other men" (Marx and Engels).

Consciousness, as we discussed in our earlier discussion, is the social product and it is the apparent form of mind. Though language is the real practical consciousness for Marx, it must be a social product that emerged from need. So the language realizes the human mind that emerges from the social conditions.

This was the brief discussion on the doctrines on the *Origin of Language* from which we can distillate the main trends of the doctrines made on the origin of language, and we would be able to present it in the further section, where we will analyze them based on the objective corresponding, that is truth condition for all the doctrines.

11
Philosophical Backgrounds of The Doctrines

We are now known to the nature, form, and types of Philosophy, the process of conception, development of cognition/knowledge, and the formation of doctrine. We came to know that, every doctrine is always determined by philosophy. Doctrine is an outcome of philosophy. Idealist philosophy creates the idealist outlook and idealist doctrine, and materialist philosophy provides the materialist outlook and materialist doctrine.

When we studied the process of formation of doctrine we noted that formation stages start from the perception of the objective world through human sense organs. The concrete perception turns to the abstract conception in the mind and gets memorized. It becomes intellect and enhances fantasy (imagination) and comes forward as a doctrine.

To present a true doctrine, it is a must to follow the correct process of inquiry. If the methodology of the research got biased by any factor the outcome (doctrine) will not be true.

The methodology for research plays the biggest role. It is a topic that has not been touched yet in this work. The methodology is a system of inquiry enhanced by *'outlook'*. Outlook is the point of view to see the actuality of the world and its developmentIt is always determined by philosophy. Thus, the different philosophies always have different outlooks and methodologies.

Methodology leads us to ontology and epistemology. The correct methodology leads us to correct ontology and epistemology and the false methodology leads us to the false ontology and epistemology.

> "Intended or unintended, asserted or un-asserted, the result of every study is the consequence of the application of the methodology. Only a correct methodology can present the true image of reality… The ontological basis is already contained in methodological norms and rules of acquiring knowledge. This also means that the methodology is the mode of interpreting reality"(Gupta).

Scientific methodology is a methodology that equips humans to discover the ever-changing and causally-interconnected objective reality, through practice. This is what we are talking about since our initial point of discussion, the scientific interpretation must have to correspond to the objective reality. Otherwise, the outlook and outcome shall both be false.

There are two types of philosophies in general; 1. Idealism and 2. Materialism. Every known philosophy in the world despite their different names can be grouped under anyone from them according to their fundamental primary consideration, i.e. *what is the primary; Idea or Matter?* This is the fundamental question of philosophy based on which we can group them in either of the mentioned above.

The second classification of their camps under these two is based on another set of fundamental questions, indeed supplementary to the previous questions. They are; I*s the world real or not? The world is a creation or development in itself?Can it be cognized?* And *does the world change or not?* This set of questions presents the outlook of the concerned philosophy.

We can fill the answer based on the previous discussion according to which the following table can be formed.

According to this table, it is the base that we extracted so far in our discussion that can be applied to the doctrines on the 'Origin of Language'. The interpretation of every phenomenon comes through above mentioned fundamental questions. Then it is obvious that the doctrines of the origin of language can be analyzed based on these fundamental questions. While investigating the problem of the origin of language, all the research depends on the investigators' methodological starting-point and the aims for which the investigation has been planed.

We have discussed the various doctrines on the origin of language. The brief data made us enable, that we can categorize them into groups based on their philosophical backgrounds. That we do in further discussion.

Philosophy	Idealism	Materialism
What is Primary?	Idea	Matter
Is the world is real or not?	No, it is not real. Or No, is just a reflection of the real ideal world	Yes, it is real, there is no other ideal world.
The world is a creation or not?	Yes, the World is the creation of external power.	No, The world is a developing matter.
Can it be cognized?	No, it can never be cognized. All the knowledge that we have is false.	Yes, it can be cognized through our sense organs. But no abstract conception takes place. Through concrete perception, abstract conception takes place.
Does the world change or not?	No, changes never happen. It changes but, controlled by the almighty, ideal, will, etc.	Yes, it changes. But it is a circular motion path only, change is mechanical. It changes in a spiral motion path only, and dialectical change happens.

Now let us first identify the main trends of the doctrines based on the previous discussion.

Trends in the Doctrines

We know the language – as in the sense we know it – is unique to humans. No one of the communication systems that exist in the other animals despite even the involvement of sounds to communicate, can be called 'Language'. A hoot of an owl, the dance of a bee, and a grunt of a pig have a huge difference from a person reciting a poem of Faiz Ahmed Faiz.

As we mentioned that the doctrines on the *origin of language* determined by different philosophies, of course, have different beliefs for the origin of language. These differences are definite and can be seen clearly as they exit due to philosophical differences.

Some of them advocate imitational origin of language, some said language is naturally originated without any human effort, some say it is gifted by God, some apply big-bang doctrine on origin of language, some said language originated from the tower of babel, some says language origin takes place from the social need of the humans, According to some proponents primary function of language is not to communicate, and the anatomy of the humans are not to produce speech. Some scholars said that the source of the language in humans is human labour and human themselves are the product of labor.

So let us discuss these assertions in general to mark the main trends of the doctrines.

Some views on the origin of language show uncertainty, most of the literature available on the topic seems to follow the trend that; they talk about the divine origin of language, then on imitating and funny named doctrines; Bow! Bow! & Pooh! Pooh! etc. and then move to the evolutionary view of the origin of language and conclude that this problem can't be answered.

"Of course, holes still remain in our knowledge: in particular, at what stage did language leap from being something new which humans discovered to being something which every newborn human is scheduled to acquire? This is still a puzzle"(Aitchison).

A text, named 'The Origin of Language' by Edward Vajda propagates the same confusion. In which he first talked about the divine view of the origin of language. He then claims that this hypothesis is impossible to prove but also not possible to disapprove due to the probable existence of primitive languages at some point in human history. The same he did about the so-called Bow! Bow! & Pooh! Pooh! Doctrines.

Then he seems to agree that the invention of language is the result of human brain development and at some point in history, humans evolved the capacity of acquiring language. Gestures were the primary conditions of the creative language system. He claims that the natural evolution hypothesis; the biological, and neurological capacities were developed first, and the meaning assigning in cultural development is the aftermath process. But soon, he again asserts this hypothesis can also not be proven.

He follows the famous trend in which writers try to show that they are not sure about the origin of language. How do humans devise their language? Is the question to which they attempt to bypass to refract the attention of others. Regardless of its origin. He talked about the language origin as an invention view in the text but as the usual trend in this text, he is not sure about anything for this type of invention. About every doctrine discussed in this text; the writer has the position; "…it can't be approved, but it can't be disapproved"(Vajda).

By this, there is a conscious attack on the social existence of language, and all of the energy has been put to prove language as not a human social characteristic.

While examining this type of text, we find that the writers seem very confused in their subjectivity. Their subjective conceptions that the language origin is a mystical phenomenon do not let the asserters go beyond this. Whenever they went to discuss the basis of some objective facts, they were pulled back by their subjectivity.

They referred to the language-teaching experiments on animals like chimpanzees, as they start to understand some meanings in communication. On basis of that, they try to assert that the language is common to all animals including humans. This trend aims only to distort the studies on the origin of language because it does neither try to prove any doctrine true nor try to prove any of them false but just only to play a wicked role.

There is another trend found in the studies that states language has just biological roots, and the function of speech organs is not to produce speech.

Accordingly, Language evolved as an exaptation of the process; in which features acquire function for they were not originally adapted. Thus, according to them "...language is first and foremost a modelling system and that only in a second stage it has been redeployed as a verbal communication system"(Barbieri).

This view empowers the universal grammar view, in which humans have the innate tendency to acquire the language, which gets triggered by a small set of inputs and produces an infinite number of outputs. This is the famous view of the innate language faculty held by Chomsky. According to him, language faculty is a component of the intellect and moral nature of man and all the natural properties require an *'agency'* to exist.

According to Chomsky, language originated rapidly due to rewiring, which happened in the brain. This incident according to him happened in Africa, from where the ancestors of humans, not yet departed, were residing (see Chomsky, "Three Factors"). The 'promising', 'world-wide accepted' linguistics considers this so-called 'human capacity; a mystery as he said, requires 'some other's influence, law, or, agency' to exist.

His universal grammar is a concept of descendant

language, on which all the world languages are based. The conception of *I-language* is similar to that base language. A sudden change caused the emergence of language in humans, syntax appeared automatically. According to him every concept and word is mind-dependent by which he believes the abstraction first and denied the primacy of practice by denying the role of experience.

It is a trend to prove language origin as a sudden phenomenon and the doctrine of the sudden origin of language leads to its divine origin. As we discussed earlier that the religious texts held the created and gifted view of the origin of life and the origin of language as well.

In the doctrine of the divine origin of language. God created the whole of the world and created the first human. God gifted him the language to name everything. That was the 'first language.' This language was once the language spoken at the *'tower of babel'*. From where the scattering of humans and language took place and languages started becoming different from the first language.

According to Hewes, the view that the language emerged through a wholly natural process among the humans who had similar cognitive power to the modern man. This view seems not to consider the human efforts to develop language. And accepting the same cognition ability at the time of language origin as humans have today is also seems hard (see Hewes et al.).

An almost similar view was given by the Suessmilch in which he created a paradox between the thought emerged first or the language emerged first? as there can be no language without thought and the existence of thought depends on the prior existence of language. He concluded that the only solution to this paradox is to presume the language as a gift by god. What a simple way to propose unscientific assertions in the name of a gift.

The 'Bow-Bow' doctrine of the origin of language by Max Müller is the doctrine of the onomatopoeic origin of language. According to which language originated from the imitation of the sounds of the animals. Pooh-Pooh doctrine held the view that the origin of language had emotional roots and it originated from the instinctive human cries. Ding-Dong doctrine considers the harmonic necessity as the cause of the language origin just as the bell has the struck sound, leaves have the cracking sound, and humans have language. Work chant doctrine has the view that the chants in the accompanying labor gave rise to the origin of language. La-La doctrine has the view that love songs and poetic sensibility originated the language in humans. Gestural and oral+gesture doctrine both consider the roots of language origin in physiological gestures following which the speech-language originated.

Berezin termed these funny-name doctrines as *pseudoscientific* doctrines. He mentioned the impossibility of building a theory of the origin of language on the imitation doctrine. Imitative sounds can relate to the natural processes producing sounds so they can't represent silent phenomena. He also criticized the gestural doctrine, as he said no people on the earth use gesture language, primarily or exclusively as their mode of communication. According to him, it is true that the gesture system is supplementary to the language.

From the point of view of practical life—and after all, that is what matters here—the unscientific theory of the priority of gesture language is really absurd, because this would have allowed communication only with people in the immediate neighbourhood, necessarily excluding conversation with people at a distance or in the dark"(Berezin).

He also wrote about the work chant doctrine of Ludwig Noire; according to which the origin of language regarding the labor activities of man and stated the origin of language in the rhythmical cries or sounds made by a human group during the course of common work, *e.g.* as sailors drawing a boat. Berezin said none of these doctrines give sufficient solutions to the question of the origin of language.

Johann Herder considered language origin through

the innate capacity to acquire language and denied both the divine and the invention view of the origin of language.

Rousseau held the inventions doctrine where emotive cries and gestures were pre-speech human communication systems that they found insufficient as the need of abstraction. Thus, they invented language.

Lieberman despite his evolutionary cloak, considers the gifted view for the origin of language. According to him, humans did special modifications in their vocal tracts to produce speech. He held the view that humans developed speech as a tool. He advocates universal grammar and the innate capacity responsible to learn the language.

Michel Corballis states that the origin of language took place gradually not rapidly. He accredited the human-bipedalism to start the creating conditions for the emergence of language.

According to Pavlov, the origin of language is a modification in the nervous system but is not a sudden modification that we saw in the case of Chomsky and others. According ro Pavlop It happened through long developmental process.

Pavlov classifies the animal communication system and the human communication system. In animals, there is a tendency of a concrete signalling system which according to Pavlov, is the first signalling system and the human communication system is the second signalling system that has the degree of abstractness. The first signalling system is also present in the human communication system. But the second signalling system is unique to the human brain. Hence language is unique to humans. But the fundamental laws that govern the first signalling system also govern the second signalling system. Because it is the activity of the same nervous tissue.

This statement by the well-known physiologist of the world put breaks to the extra wiring, immediate modification, and special chromosomal change suggestions in humans for the doctrine of the origin of language.

According to Engels; "First labour, after it and then with it speech – these were the two most essential stimuli under the influence of which the brain of the ape gradually changed into that of man, which, for all its similarity is far larger and more perfect"(Engels, *Transition from Ape to Man*).

According to this statement, it is said that the language is not a property that appeared in the humans that were like modern humans. But appeared in apes and before the language, it was labor; that appeared. Both of these influenced the development of the brain of the ape, by which it gradually developed.

As we also mention that without language, i.e. the stage of consciousness, no further stages of cognition and knowledge are possible. So language plays the biggest role in human epistemology. But before language there is the human practice, there is the human 'labour'.

According to Engels Erect posture and human practice made them so close to each other, that they need to say something to each other, emerged. This necessity transformed the undeveloped larynx into a developed vocal organ. He referred, this advancement as the *'the law of correlation growth'* as proposed by Charles Darwin.

Karl Marx also termed language as social practical consciousness and considered its emergence from the social need of communicational intercourse. He said it exists for me because it exists for others.

We can extract the main trends from this brief discussion easily. The data can be seen in contradictory oppositions.

Because on the one side some of these doctrines; considered language origin as a gift from God, but on the other side, there is an outlook that does not consider it as a gift on divine creation but believes in the evolutionary emergence of language.

Some of them consider the rapid, immediate, once a time emergence of fully developed language aftermath of a so-called *big-bang*. That is considered by them as the terminus point in the history of the world. It holds the view of pure biological emergence of language by denying its social emergence, according to them, language emerged in humans by the emergence of an innate capacity of language faculty. Whose cause of emergence is not certain and can't be analyzed. This trend leads to universal grammar and the monogenetic emergence of language.

But on the other way, some of them consider the language as a gradually developed system for communication. Accordingly, it is a nervous change in humans but not rapid but a gradual development in which the human ability of language i.e. unique to humans, originated. The modification of the anatomy was caused by the development of their erect posture and the free movement of hands, which on the one hand, repositioned the vocal-box and the practice of labor by hands, made the conditions to conceptualize the world and to develop the abstract concepts more rapidly. But it never took place through a sudden emergence. This trend leads to the social emergence of language.

But there is a trend that believes in evolution but also accepts the sudden emergence of language, considers the importance of language in the thought process, but asserts that the language could not emerge without the prior-developed thought. The answer they give to the "self-created paradox" is that some prior power gifted the language to them.

We aimed to extract the main tendencies in the doctrines on the origin of language that we have almost done. So according to these considerations, we can now proceed to classify them into main trends. The common classification for these trends is available widely in four, in which they can be classified as follows:

- Divine Origin
- The natural sound source origin
- The origin through genetic change and
- The origin through Physical Adaptation

But the following classification of them into seven can be seen:
- Divine Origin
- The natural sound source origin
- The Social-Interaction origin
- The tool-making origin
- The origin through genetic change
- The origin through Physical Adaptation
- The Doctrine of Social Necessity

So these seven trends are commonly known in the studies of the origin of language can be reduced into two, based on their emergence, i.e. Sudden vs Gradual. **Doctrines of Sudden Emergence**

CHARACTERISTICS OF THE TRENDS OF DOCTRINES ON 'THE ORIGIN OF LANGUAGE'			
Doctrines	Source	Development	Monogenetic
Divine Origin	God/Creator/Legislator	Sudden	Yes
The Natural Sound Source Origin	Imitation of Natural/Animal Sounds	Gradual	--
The Interactional Origin	Work Chants	Gradual	--
The Tool-Making Origin	Making of tools enhanced speech dependency	Gradual	--
The Origin Through Genetic Change	Innate Language Faculty/Universal Grammar	Sudden	Yes
The Origin Through Physical Adaptation	Development of Human Anatomy	Gradual	No
The Origin due to Social Necessity	Evolution - Leaps - Evolution	Gradual + Rapid	No
Evolutionary with Terminus Point	Gifted + Evolution	Sudden + Gradual	Yes

These are the doctrines that believe the emergence of the human ability to produce language took place suddenly, without any historic development, humans started speaking.

The doctrine of the divine origin, genetic origin i.e. the language as a gift of God, and the language emerged from the genetic rewiring, and evolutionary with Terminus Point, according to which language is developing based on evolution. But it could not be started by itself, it must be a gift for humans.

Doctrines of Gradual Emergence:

Thisis the view that contradicts the doctrines of the sudden doctrine for the emergence of language. It considers the gradual development in human anatomy. By which they developed the ability of the production of speech for communication. The advanced development includes the development of hands, postures, speech anatomy, brain, and the development of cognition and knowledge as well.

Hence we can group the hitherto discussed doctrines under two categories according to their tendencies on the question of emergence. From these trends, we can move forward to analyze the philosophical backgrounds of the doctrine of the origin of language.

CLASSIFICATION OF DOCTRINES OF THE BASIS OF THEIR VIEW ON THE EMERGENCE OF LANGUAGE	
Sudden Emergence	*Gradual Origin*
Divine Origin The Origin Through Genetic Change Evolutionary with Terminus Point	The Natural Sound Source Origin The Interactional Origin The Tool-making Origin The Origin Through Physical Adaptation The origin due to Social Necessity

The Philosophical background of the doctrines on the origin of language

So far we know, how philosophy determines our decisions, what are the epistemological roots of the making of doctrine and we are attempted to analyze the philosophical aspects from the beginning of the work. As the continuation here we will discuss the philosophical backgrounds of the trends of the doctrines, we got from our discussion so far.

We classified the doctrines based on the most frequently exclusive factor, *i.e.* the time span consideration for the origin of language, do they consider sudden origin or gradual origin.

From now onwards in our further discussion, philosophical backgrounds of the main trends of these doctrines. We know behind every doctrine, there is a philosophy. It can either be Idealist or Materialist. We can categories these doctrines between philosophies of **Idealism** and **Materialism.**

Before proceeding next chapter to do so we have to keep in mind the debate between these two philosophical camps of Idealism and Materialism and their considerations. It is also important to recall the further classification in these philosophies. By this, we will have an understanding of what basis they stand on and we would be able to subgroup the doctrine also.

12

Idealist Doctrines

Philosophy of Idealism considers the primacy of Ideas over the Matter. Proponents of Idealism do not consider the world as a self-developing objective reality but consider it as the reflection, creation, false world, will, an ego, etc. Accordingly, there is an external agency that has control over the world, and all the objects, humans, are the creation of a creator, legislator, non-ego, absolute idea, etc. So these doctrines for the origin of language can be grouped under the idealist doctrines. First, we have to sub-classify the Idealist camp as we mentioned earlier.

By using the considerations, mentioned in the table given below, anyone can easily state that the doctrines of the sudden emergence of the origin of language can be grouped under the idealist camp.

By using this information to propose the background of the doctrines from extracted main trends. It is easy to place two doctrines i.e. doctrine of divine origin and evolutionary + terminus point, doctrines from the mentioned three of the doctrines of sudden emergence, under the Idealist doctrines. Whereas in the case of the origin through genetic change seems difficult in the first look, to place in Idealist camp because of its pseudo-scientific cloak, i.e. so-called genetic change and change in chromosomal information, change in DNA structure, and many more assertions without mentioning the social emergence or even social existence of language. But the phenomenon of sudden emergence, consideration of universal grammar, and innate faculty of language place it under the idealist camp for sure. The point of discussion is; In which camp of idealism they can be categorized? Let us analyze it in further discussion.

Subjective Idealist Doctrines

Divine origin doctrine, by the consideration of the gift of full-fledged language from the very beginning, along with this considering the *first-language* conception and *tower of babel* as the source of the first language exposes its subjectivity. So the doctrine of the divine origin of language is a Subjective Idealist doctrine.

The next doctrine of the origin through genetic change considers universal grammar and the innateness of language. The doctrine of Noam Chomsky is also subjective. Let us see what Corballis said;

> "Chomsky's theory has remarkable parallels with the biblical account. I-language may be likened to the universal language that God gave to Adam, and E-languages to the babble of tongues that emerged after the destruction of the Tower of Babel. Indeed Chomsky might have been tempted to call the lucky recipient of I-language Adam rather than Prometheus—although he was perhaps prophetic, since Prometheus is the Greek word for forethought! Linguists are as much in dispute about the nature of I-language, or universal grammar, as were theologians about the nature of the original tongue. Chomsky's theory also has an element of Platonic idealism, and indeed of heavenly perfection, in that unbounded Merge is an ideal, a "perfect" device for creating thought processes underlying the babble of actual languages that infest the globe. The mapping of I-language onto E-language is referred to as "externalization," and it is in this process that the

imperfections and messiness of the world's languages arise. I-language may perhaps be likened to gravity, an elegant principle that explains why objects fall to the ground when dropped" (Corballis, The Truth about Language).

	Camps of Idealism	
	Subjective Idealism	**Objective Idealism**
Existence of World	It is not real, and only a reflection of an Ideal-Universal World. There are no objects without subjects. Objects are the combinations of our sensations e.g. I think therefore I exist	It exists, but always under the control of power, without the will of which even a leaf can't move.
Change/Development	Change does not happen. Change can violate universality.	Objects once created by the almighty, remain under the change, according to his will. They acquire everything, according to his will.
Can the world be cognized?	No	It can be. But the knowledge we get through our senses is always false. Our mind can give us true knowledge

The universality of I-Language, its idealization as the perfect language, and the imperfection of E-language are the testimonies of his Idealist outlook, along with the spreading hypothesis for world languages, the sudden emergence of language capacity, and considering speech anatomy not especially evolved for language function demotes man from the creator of language by asserting humans incapable to acquire language based on experience. These are the main postulations of Chomsky and Chomskyan. It is the subjective idealist cloak of our time in the name of modern linguistics. This doctrine is as unscientific as the *divine origin* doctrine is. Thus, the Subjective Idealist doctrines are not only anti-social and anti-science but are anti-human and anti-society, indeed.

Objective Idealist Doctrine:

The doctrine considers the existence of the objective world, but always under the control of power, without the will of which, even a leaf can't move. All Objects are the creation of almighty, those once created, remain under the change, according to its (Almighty's) will. They acquire everything, every new property according to his will. The world can be cognized. But the knowledge we get through our senses is always false. Only our minds can give us true knowledge.

By just calculating the result of the objective idealist equation. We will get extraction that there is a power who created all things including humans, gave language as a gift to humans because nothing can happen without its will, every new property is a change commanded by the almighty.

So accordingly language could be developed gradually but language; the most complex and sophisticated phenomenon in humans couldn't emerge on its own. It must need a creator to be so. According to Lieberman, humans have been developed special modifications in their vocal tract to produce speech, organs of speech were especially evolved for the production of speech. But as he said, "Speech is so essential to our concept of intelligence that its possession is virtually equated with being human. Animals who talk are human, because what sets us apart from other animals is the 'gift' of speech" (Lieberman, Eve Spoke), is the best presentation of objective idealism in which a proponent accepts the evolution of language on one hand and stating it as a gift on the other.

Thus, philosophical outlooks of Idealism believe in creation in one or the other way. The Idealist doctrines on the origin of language consider human language as a creation or gift by an external power that controls all things including man and their language.

13

Materialist Doctrines

Materialist Philosophy considers Matter as primary, and it is eternal according to them. The idea is secondary and emerges after the cognition of the material world by the mind through human senses, which itself is a product of the process of cognition. Advocates of materialism consider the world as a self-developing objective reality and do not even consider any assertion about its creation by any external agencies.

We have already discussed earlier that Materialism does also have two camps further based on their considerations about the change in matter, i.e. materialistic motion in direction and mode of the motion. Which split them into three, viz. Materialism-Spontaneous, Materialism-Metaphysical, and Materialism-Dialectical. Let us try to understand their split with the table given on the next page.

Materialism-Spontaneous Doctrines

Materialism spontaneous had a very guess-based interpretation of the world, these materialists were clear that no creation of world happened ever, and it is a self-developing substance. But they could make only guesses about that substance. Which they consider basic in the formation of the world.

A similar tendency of considering, one basic guess-based cause for language origin can be seen in the natural-sound source origin (Bow-Bow, Pooh-Pooh, Ding-Dong). Although materialism spontaneous was an ancient considered phenomenon and these doctrines under our analysis appeared much later in history, the point of similarity between them is their guess-based materialist foundation and no consideration to the creationist hypothesis.

	Materialism-Spontaneous	Materialism-Metaphysical	Materialism-Dialectical
Existence of World	The world is real and made up of one basic substance, i.e. Air, Water, Apeiron, etc.	It exists and Matter is primary. And no one created it.	It exists and Matter is primary. And no one created it.
Change and Development	Everything is changing in itself. Dialectics is the cause of all change.	Change is mechanical and, Changes are repetitive in a circular motion.	Change is dialectical, It follows a spiral path, And changes according to the three laws of Dialectical motion.
Can the world be cognized?	Yes.	It can be cognized through senses. But only basic sensation can be acquired. No abstract conception takes place.	It can be cognized through sense organs. Through concrete perception, abstract conception takes place. Objective world+human practice develops cognition+knowledge which further enhances human practice.

These are guess-based doctrines because their proponents were confused about the cause of the origin of language. Even Max Müller, the proponent of several spontaneous doctrines, could not be able to clear himself for this, he proposed doctrines based on imitation basis, i.e. onomatopoeic doctrine. The onomatopoeic doctrines assume a causal connection between the origin of speech and the purely sensory impression of the sounds of nature. Although every language of the world contains some onomatopoeic characteristics. But considering the origin of language from this is as subjective as the divine origin doctrine.

Indian spontaneous studies also contain statements on the origin and framing of language on an onomatopoeic basis. Sneh Prabha Madan, in a paper entitled *The Origin and Nature of Language,*' mentioned the Indian spontaneous doctrines; In India, The existence of onomatopoeic words is a factor responsible for forming language. 'Yāska' accepted this principle of 'onomatopoeia' i.e. 'Anukarna' as a phenomenon of language. 'Pāṇini' too, clearly stated 'Anukarna' i.e. imitation, as a factor responsible for the formation of words. According to Yāska ''onomatopoeia' is mostly found in the names of birds. The word 'Dundubhi' as explained by him refers to the onomatopoeical character of the early words: 'Dundubhiriti' 'sabadanukaranam'''(*see* Madan).

The lack of scientific information has led these proponents in the wrong ways and these funny named doctrines appeared in history. But a detailed study and mature outlook can overthrow these cloaks.

Materialism-Metaphysical Doctrines

Materialism Metaphysical in opposition to Idealism was very rigid for its primary consideration denying the phenomenon abstraction. They held the view that the material world is the only reality, and there is no creation of the world ever happened. Thus, the idealist approach is a lie. Opposing idealism led them to rigidly resist the abstraction of phenomena in the mind, they only accept sensual perception and do not consider the human mind as a reflector of reality because they were against considering it a projector.

This assumption led the followers of this view on the origin of language to consider the 'work-chant' origin and gestural origin doctrine. Which considers language, not as an abstract phenomenon but a simple interactional and reflexive phenomenon. This view is not an advocate for human practice as a key phenomenon of human development. That's why they remained unable to overcome the real loop. According to Suman Gupta; a sufficiently developed brain granted the appearance of a new pattern of behaviors; implies, the organisms when it attains a given complexity develops new qualities which cannot be reduced to physiological reflexes (*see* Gupta).

Thus, the origin of language was a qualitative change in humans that was caused by the developed brain generated by the human practice, the reduction of the origin of language solely to gestures doctrine, (physical reflexes) can never be right.

> "It may seem at first glance that Noire's theory is essentially materialistic because it is also connected with labour to some extent. But it differs from Engels's theory in that it considers that speech accompanied labour whereas Engels held that labour created speech. It is futile to ask whether man or language came into existence first. The two are inseparably interrelated; each presupposes the other" (Berezin).

Thus, the Metaphysical and Spontaneous outlooks did not have that capacity that could be able to explain the real cause behind the origin of any human phenomenon because they did not arrive at the level where they could see humans as a creation of their practice. Objective conditions enabled man to invent Labour. The tool-making ability, a decisivequalitative step resulted from the gradual quantitative development, further enforced qualitative changes. This process of motion was not acquired by the Metaphysical materialists.

Behaviorist doctrines are also the outcomes of the philosophy that do not consider any discontinuity between animal communication and human language. Behaviorism reduces humans to their animal functions and denies the essential human qualitative differentiative characteristics, those are, the social being of humans and the social necessity to fulfill their needs. They consider man alike the other organisms in nature, who receive stimuli from their environment, and respond to individual stimuli accordingly. We can see this tendency in Skinner and other behaviorists. Who reduces human cognition and knowledge to the simple absorption (spirit), reflection (soul) phenomena as we discussed earlier in this work, their assumption of *'blank slate'* state of mind and only response based doctrine is an *'anti-abstraction'* doctrine.

The right philosophical outlook which interprets the origin of language is none other than the dialectical materialist doctrines, about we are on the verse to discuss.

Materialism Dialectical Doctrines

Although humans are part of nature, but still they are qualitatively advanced than the rest of organisms. This qualitative difference is produced by the long eternal chain of quantitative and qualitative changes. Humans have a materialist existence; constituted of mechanical, physical, chemical and biological processes that follow the mechanical, physical, chemical, and biological laws. But when we stop just at the biological processes and biological laws, we conduct a huge theoretical mistake. Humans above of all have a social existence. Next to biological laws, there are sociological laws, this phase of human existence is different in such a way, that we found nothing beyond the social necessity as the urge of all human inventions.

Materialism-Dialectical is a philosophy that considers the three fundamental laws of dialectics, 1. The law of the transformation of quantity into quality and vice versa; 2. The law of the interpenetration of opposites; 3. The law of the negation of the negation. As the basis of the development of matter as well as thought. Lenin in an article entitled; *'Karl Marx',* wrote about these laws of development, as follows;

"A development that repeats, as it were, stages that

have already been passed, but repeats them in a different way, on a higher basis ("the negation of negation"), a development, so to speak, that proceeds in spirals, not in a straight line; a development by leaps, catastrophes, and revolutions; "breaks in continuity"; the transformation of quantity into quality; inner impulses towards development, imparted by the contradiction and conflict of the various forces and tendencies acting on a given body, or within a given phenomenon, or within a given society; the interdependence and the closest and indissoluble connection between all aspects of any phenomenon (history constantly revealing ever new aspects), a connection that provides a uniform, and universal process of motion, one that follows definite laws—these are some of the features of dialectics as a doctrine of development that is richer than the conventional one"(Lenin, "Karl Marx").

No phenomenon or object in the world exists in the isolation, they have an interdependent, dialectical relation with each other. The development of nature and society is caused by these three laws of development. The development follows a spiral path according to Lenin. This understanding as a whole appears as a Dialectical and Historical Materialist outlook. Let us also have a look at Stalin's understanding of this.

"Dialectical materialism is the world outlook of the [Materialism]. It is called dialectical materialism because its approach to the phenomena of nature, its method of studying and apprehending them, is dialectical, while its interpretation of the phenomena of nature, its conception of these phenomena, its theory, is materialistic. Historical materialism is the extension of the principles of dialectical materialism to the study of social life, an application of the principles of dialectical materialism to the phenomena of the life of society, to the study of society and of its history" (Stalin).

Dialectical Materialism is the materialist outlook to study the development of nature, whereas historical materialism measures the development of society. This is how the laws and outlook for human society differ from laws and outlook for nature, despite being fundamentally the same. Historical Materialism is the advancement in Dialectical Materialism. Thus, the outlook of the Materialist (dialectical) philosophy is dialectical and historical materialism. Dialectics is the doctrine of development in its fullest, deepest, and most comprehensive form, the doctrine of the relativity of human knowledge that provides us with a reflection of eternally developing matter. The development of cognition and knowledge.

"In one point, however, the history of the development of society turns out to be essentially different from that of nature. In nature—in so far as we ignore man's reverse action upon nature—there are only blind, unconscious agencies acting upon one another, out of whose interplay the general law comes into operation." (Engels, "End of Classical German Philosophy").

The essence of man is a social being who aspires, plans, and changes its concrete objective condition by acquiring knowledge of laws of development of the objective world. i.e. Nature and its own society.

The origin of language according to Materialism (Dialectical) is not sudden and not the creation of almighty. It has been developed from the social need for communication. It is a real practical consciousness according to Marx and the consciousness is a product of human practice, in the process of developing cognition and knowledge.

As the comment of Berezin; we mentioned the doctrine of Noire, expresses the basic difference between a metaphysical and dialectical doctrine as Noire's doctrine is metaphysical; that doesn't consider *'Labour'* as the creator of human phenomena, including speech. But historical materialism asserts that the speech is a creation of Labour.

"Materialism does not consider language an abstract creation of scholars or lexicologists but as something arising out of labour and practical needs of countless generations of Mankind"(Berezin). Thus, the language is the creation of labour and practice of mankind, and humans themselves are the creation of their labour. Labour transforms them to be humans through the eternal dialectical process. Engels mentioned in *Dialectical Materialism* is the cor appropriate example for an actual outlook to analyze and explain dialectical objective reality, as follows;

"But it is precisely dialectics that constitutes the most important form of thinking for present-day natural science, for it alone offers the analogue for, and thereby the method of explaining, the evolutionary processes occurring in nature, inter-connections in general, and transitions from one field of investigation to another" (Engels, *Dialectics of Nature - 1886*).

There are only dialectics that offers the correct method to explaining the evolutionary processes occurring in nature and society. Materialists of this type praised Darwin's theory of natural selection as a victory of materialism, as it presented the scientific foundation of human evolution from "lower" animals. Darwin's theory of the origin of species is rooted in the natural material sciences, not in theology or metaphysics. Natural selection itself is a dialectical process.

The origin of language is an emergence of an advanced property in mankind.Quantitative evolutionary changes that happened in apes produced a qualitatively different species. Humans are the only animal that undertook Labour - a conscious conflict with nature, they purposefully changed nature for their advantage but also changed themselves through in the same process simultaneously.

"Labour is the source of all wealth..." Engels said, "...But it is even infinitely more than thisIt is the prime basic condition for all human existence, and this to such an extent that, in a sense, we have to say that labour created man himself" (Engels, *Transition from Ape to Man*). Hence according to these materialists doctrines, human labour is responsible for the origin of language.

The erect posture of apes allowed them to free their hands to first to use the tools for their advantage and then to make the tools. This was the decisive step in the transition from apes to humans. The hand is the organ of Labour and according to Engels,

> "Thus, the hand is not only the organ of labour, it is also the product of labour. Only by labour, by adaptation to ever new operations, through the inheritance of muscles, ligaments, and, over longer periods of time, bones that had undergone special development and the ever-renewed employment of this inherited finesse in new, more and more complicated operations, have given the human hand the high degree of perfection required to conjure into being the pictures of a Raphael, the statues of a Thorwaldsen, the music of a Paganini"(*ibid.*).

The development of hand for Labour from Labour, is resulted from human practice which enhanced cognition and knowledge development. Perfection in practice for concrete operations built the mind; the *'capacity'* in the human brain that holds the abstract conceptions of the concrete objective reality of the world.

> "Mastery over nature began with the development of the hand, with labour, and widened man's horizon at every new advance. He was continually discovering new, hitherto unknown properties in natural objects. On the other hand, the development of labour necessarily helped to bring the members of society closer together by increasing cases of mutual support and joint activity, and by making clear the advantage of this joint activity to each individual. In short, men in the making arrived at the point where they had something to say to each other. Necessity created the organ; the undeveloped larynx of the ape was slowly but surely transformed by modulation to produce

constantly more developed modulation, and the organs of the mouth gradually learned to pronounce one articulate sound after another"(*ibid*).

According to this doctrine, labour enlarged the human horizon at every new advance and bring the members of society close together by mutual support and joint activity. It was human Labour that transformed apes into the man. Labour is also the cause behind the origin of language. In essence, Labour is the creator of all human phenomena. This doctrine believes that the social necessity of communication is responsible for the origin of language. The tool making doctrine, Physical adaptation doctrine, work-chant doctrine, onomatopoeic doctrine, gestural origin doctrine, all notwithstanding their material assumptions did not reach the central basic cause for the origin of language due to their absurd outlook, that merely allowed them to assert guess based assumptions instead of the correct interpretation.

Engels in the same work mentioned above refers to Darwin's *'Law of Co-relation of Growth'* as "…the body benefited from the law of correlation of growth,".

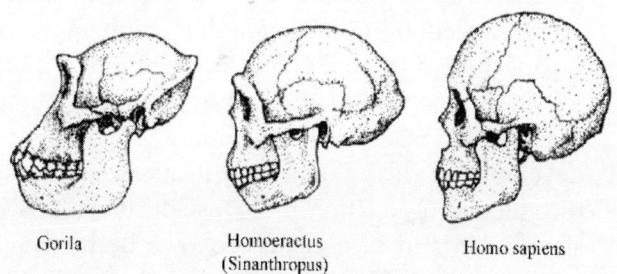

Brain size comparison
https://www.ling.upenn.edu/courses/Fall_2016/ling001/boule_skulls.gif

"This law states that the specialised forms of separate parts of an organic being are always bound up with certain forms of other parts that apparently have no connection with them…Changes in certain forms involve changes in the form of other parts of the body, although we cannot explain the connection.

Perfectly white cats with blue eyes are always, or almost always, deaf. The gradually increasing perfection of the human hand, and the commensurate adaptation of the feet for erect gait, have undoubtedly, by virtue of such correlation, reacted on other parts of the organism" (*ibid.*)

The correlational growth in organisms is the condition that transforms not only the function of existing organs or arises advanced properties but also advances the organs to acquire new features. The advancement and perfection of the human hand is such a prime example of the presentation of the law of correlational growth.

"...First labour, after it and then with it speech—these were the two most essential stimuli under the influence of which the brain of the ape gradually changed into that of man, which for all its similarity is far larger and more perfect. Hand in hand with the development of the brain went the development of its most immediate instruments—the sensesJust as the gradual development of speech is inevitably accompanied by a corresponding refinement of the organ of hearing, so the development of the brain as a whole is accompanied by a refinement of all the senses. The reaction on labour and speech of the development of the brain and its attendant senses, of the increasing clarity of consciousness, power of abstraction and of conclusion, gave both labour and speech an ever-renewed impulse to further development. This development did not reach its conclusion when man finally became distinct from the ape, but on the whole made further powerful progress, its degree and direction varying among different peoples and at different times, and here and there even being interrupted by local or temporary regression. This further development has been strongly urged forward, on the one hand, and guided along more definite directions, on the other, by a new element which came into play with the appearance of fully-fledged man, namely, society" *(ibid)*.

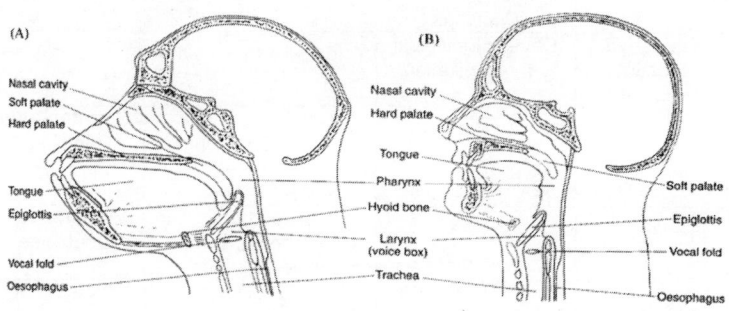

Comparison of human and chimpanzee vocal-tract anatomy
https://www.ling.upenn.edu/courses/Fall_2016/ling001/twoheads.gif

This was how the change in the use of hands transformed the anatomy of humans. Thus, the law of co-relational growth lowered the human voice box at such a position suitable to articulate sound and the developing cognition and knowledge enable humans to speak according to Materialism-Dialectical. "By the combined functioning of hand, speech organs and brain, not only in each individual but also in society, men became capable of executing more and more complicated operations, and were able to set themselves, and achieve, higher and higher aims" *(ibid)*. The objective circumstances humans are responsible for the all transformation.

This was the discussion about the Philosophical backgrounds of the doctrines on the origin of language, through which we analyzed how different philosophies produce different types of doctrines on the same type of problem. This is due to the different outlooks determined by the concerned philosophies which extract different outcomes.

	Idealist Doctrine	Materialist Doctrines	
Subjective Idealist Doctrines	Divine Origin Doctrines, Universal Grammar/ Language faculty Doctrines		
Objective Idealist Doctrines	Genetic/Biological Characterization.		
		Bow-Bow, Pooh-Pooh, Ding-dong Doctrines (Onametapoeic)	Spontaneous Doctrines
		work-chant, behaviorist, Blank Slate doctrines	Metaphysical Doctrines
		Social Need+labor+Physical Adaptation+congintion and knowledge development doctrines (Objective Doctrines)	Dialectical Doctrines

We classified these doctrines according to their philosophical backgrounds. Because of their philosophical determination, their truth value is subject to their objective correspondence. We know very well that every research has to be objectively correct. Until then, no doctrine can be recognized as theory.

Afterword

A lot of difference can be seen in the different doctrines on the same problem, this difference between the doctrines is due to the difference in their determining philosophies because every doctrine is philosophically determined. This difference gets develop due to their outlook to analyze the natural and social phenomena; outlook is the base for the method of inquiry by which every phenomenon in the universe can be analyzed. If an outlook considers the creation of the world from an Ideal; then it's obvious the origin of speech will also be considered as a creation not evolved. On the contrary, if an outlook believes that the world is an ever-changing matter, which develops dialectically, and thought as the product of the reflection of the objective world; then it will assert the origin of speech as a new property in human beings as the result of material circumstances. So doctrine is the ultimate product of philosophy and it can either be Idealistic or Materialistic. They both are contradictory, no doctrine can be of both types. This is due to the contradiction of the philosophies of Idealism and Materialism.

Doctrine is the product of socially developed cognition and knowledge. Which starts from the need and completes itself at the 'doctrine'. Doctrine is the highest stage of the epistemological process. Where one proposes its assertions on a given problem. This assertion can either be idealistic or materialistic depending on determining philosophy. But the truth condition of the doctrines depends on the objective correspondence. As only the true doctrines can correspond to the objective reality.

Thus, the truth or false condition of doctrine can only be analyzed by its corresponding to the objective reality and a doctrine fulfills the truth condition if and only if it interprets the objective reality. Only the objectively proved doctrine can be called theory.

Term *'Doctrine'* can be defined asthe postulation/assertions and the proposed solution by us for a given problem. In the epistemological process 'Doctrine' stands at the highest stage of developing cognition and developing knowledge.In this work, we discussed the formation of doctrine and its epistemological basis and arrived at the decision that every doctrine is determined by the philosophical approach of the proponent. Based on philosophy, there can be two types of doctrines for every problem, i.e.

1. Idealist doctrine, and
2. Materialist doctrine.

The idealist doctrine is based on the *'Creationist'* view, in which proponents believe that the world is a creation of divine power and ultimately believe language as a gift of god for humans and preachthe sudden origin of language. The other doctrine; the materialist doctrine does not consider anything as a creation of any divine power but considers dialectics as the basis of all changes including the origin of life and origin of language as well. The dialectics, in this case, is materialist-dialectics and eternal as like as the matter is. Matter doesn't exist without dialectics and dialectics has no existence without matter.

In this analyzes of philosophical backgrounds of the doctrines of the origin of language, we find some doctrines consider the sudden emergence of language and others consider that the emergence of language as gradual. The Sudden origin doctrines are the idealist doctrines, that consider the creation, monogenesis of language, they consider actual language as impure, and propose some pure universal type of language. Language is not chiefly for communication according to them and the anatomy of speech production has not been adapted for language production.

But in the opposite considerations the doctrines with the gradual development assumption, are materialist in essence. They don't consider the creation of language by god but it is built from the social necessity of communication and human labor is the creator of the language, brain, and man. The human hand is the organ of labor and the product of labor as well. This total process is the process of correlational growth, as asserted by Darwin under the *'law of correlational growth'*

Doctrines of the Divine origin of language, and the Universal Grammar/Language faculty are subjective idealist doctrines, while the doctrines that consider language origin from genetic/biological characterization are the objective idealist doctrines.

Bow-Bow, Pooh-Pooh, Ding-dong Doctrines, and other onomatopoeic doctrines are the spontaneous-materialist doctrines, and work-chant, behaviorist and Blank Slate doctrines are the Materialist-metaphysical doctrines.

The doctrine of the origin of language, which considers Social needs, human labor (practice), physical adaptation, and cognition & knowledge development, and above these, considers labor as the creator of all human phenomena are the objective doctrines of the origin of language. This doctrine is the dialectical materialist doctrine. No consideration mentioned above for this doctrine alone could create language, it started from labor and originated with the correlational development of all of them.

Through dialectical and historical materialist outlook. We inquire about the objective model of language origin by analyzing the different assertions on the origin of language. The found doctrines can only be true on their correct objective correspondence, we consider the social necessity doctrine for the origin of language only suitable in that objective correspondence. We know many doctrines on the origin of language have direct miraculous consideration and some have the mystical consideration hidden behind their so-called scientific vocabulary. But none of them fit in the objective corresponding truth condition because nature does not develop on the miraculous and mysterious laws. It evolves through the laws of dialectical development and the social necessity doctrine is alone, that is truthful for the objective conditions and dialectical fundamental laws.

This is our consideration and we consider Materialist dialectical doctrine as the true doctrine and it can be a theory as far as the question of the origin of language concerns. But it's up to the readers to check the objectivity of this doctrine.

BIBLIOGRAPHY

Aitchison, Jean. *The Seeds of Speech: Language Origin and Evolution.* Cambridge University Press, 2000.

Ali, Maulawi Sher. *The Holy Quran Arabic Text and English Translation.* Islam International Publication Limited, 2015.

Andreyev, Igor. *Engels's "The Part Played by Labour in the Transition from Ape to Man."* Progress Publishers, 1985.

Aristotle. *The Basic Works of Aristotle.* Edited by R. McKeon, Random House Publishing Group, 2009.

Barbieri, Marcello. "On the Origin of Language A Bridge Between Biolinguistics and Biosemiotics." *Biosemiotics*, vol. 3, no. 2, 2010, pp. 201–23.

Berezin, F. M. *Lectures On Linguistics.* Higher School Publishing House, 1969.

Bhartrihari. *Vakyapadiya (Cantos 1 and 2) with English Translation.* Edited by K. Raghavan Pillai, Motilal Banarsidass, 1971.

Bloch, B., and G. L. Trager. *Outline of Linguistic Analysis.* Linguistic Society of America, 1942.

Bloomfield, Leonard. *Language (1933).* George Allen & Unwin Ltd., 1973.

Bogomolov, A. S. *History of Ancient Philosophy: Greece and Rome.* Progress Publishers, 1985.

Carstairs-Mccarthy, Andrew. "Origins of Language." *The Handbook of Linguistics*, edited by Mark Aronoff and Janie

Rees-Miller, Blackwell Publishers, 2001, pp. 1–18.

Chatterjee, Satischandra, and Dhirendramohan Datta. *An Introduction to Indian Philosophy*. University of Calcutta, 1950.

Chattopadhyay, Debiprasad. *What Is Living and What Is Dead in Indian Philosophy*. Peoples Publishing House, 1976.

Chomsky, Noam. *Aspects of the Theory of Syntax*. MIT Press, 1965.

---. "Biolinguistic Explorations: Design, Development, Evolution." *International Journal of Philosophical Studies*, vol. 15, no. 1, 2007, pp. 1–21.

---. "Some Simple Evo Devo Theses: How True Might They Be for Language?" *The Evolution of Human Language: Biolinguistic Perspectives*, edited by Richard K. Larson et al., Cambridge University Press, 2010, pp. 45–62.

---. *Syntactic Structures*. Mouton de Gruyter, 1957.

---. "Three Factors in Language Design." *Linguistic Inquiry*, vol. 36, no. 1, 2005, pp. 1–22.

Corballis, Michael C. *From Hand to Mouth: The Origins Of Language*. Princeton University Press, 2003.

---. *The Recursive Mind*. Princeton University Press, 2011.

---. *The Truth about Language*. The University of Chicago Press, 2017.

Darwin, Charles. *The Descent of Man, and Selection in Relation to Sex - 1871*. John Murray, 1901.

Diels, Hermann, and Walther Kranz. *Die Fragmente Der Vorsokratiker*. Weidmann, 1985.

Duursma, K. J. "The Tower of Babel Account Affirmed by Linguistics." *Journal of Creation*, vol. 16, no. 3, 2002, pp. 27–31.

Einstein, Albert. *Cosmic Religion*. Covici Friede, 1931.

Ejaz, Manzur. *Linguistic Follies of the Subcontinent (Challenging Indo-European Theory of Languages).* Chetna Prakashan, 2021.

Engels, Frederick. *Anti-Dühring - 1878.* Progress Publishers, 1975.

---. *Dialectics of Nature - 1886.* Progress Publishers, 1972.

---. "Ludwig Feuerbach and End of Classical German Philosophy - 1886." *Marx and Engels Collected Works, Vol. 26,* International Publishers, 1975, pp. 353–98.

---. *Socialism: Utopian and Scientific - 1880.* Progress Publishers, 1970.

---. *The Part Played by Labour in the Transition from Ape to Man - 1876.* Progress Publishers, 1952.

Fromkin, Victoria, and Robert Rodman. *An Introduction to Language.* 3rd ed., Holt, Rinehart and Winston, 1983.

Gimson, A. C. *An Introduction to the Pronunciation of English.* Edward Arnold, 1980.

Gupta, Suman. *The Origin and Theories of Linguistic Philosophy (A Marxist Point of View).* Intellectual Publishing House, 1983.

Hall, Robert Anderson. *An Essay on Language.* Chilton Books, 1968.

Harari, Yuval Noaḥ. Sapiens: A Brief History of Humankind. Translated by John Purcell and Haim Watzman, Vintage Books, 2015.

Hegel, Georg Wilhelm Friedrich. *Science of Logic - 1816.* Edited by W.H Jonathan and L.G Struthers, George Allen And Unwin Ltd, 1929.

Herder, Johann Gottfried. *Der Ursprung Der Sprache.* Berlin Academy of Sciences, 1853.

Herder, Johann Gottfried Von. "Treatise on the Origin of

Language (1772)." *Herder Philosophical Writings*, edited by Michael N. Forster, Cambridge University Press, 2002, pp. 65–164.

Hewes, Gordon W. "Introduction." *Annals of the New York Academy of Sciences*, vol. 280, no. 1, 1976, p. 3.

Hewes, Gordon W., et al. "Primate Communication and the Gestural Origin of Language." *Current Anthropology*, vol. 14, no. 1/2, 1973, pp. 5–24.

Hobbes, Thomas. *The Moral and Political Works of Thomas Hobbes of Malmesbury*. The Bavarian State Library, 1750.

Hockett, Charles F. "The Problem of Universals in Language." *Universals of Language: Report of a Conference Held At Dobbs Ferry, New York, April 13-15, 1961.*, M.I.T. Press, 1966.

Jagrup Singh. Revolutionary Philosophy. Translated by Varinder Khurana, Progress International Publishers, 2021.

Jespersen, Otto. *Language: Its Nature, Development, and Origin*. G. Allen & Unwin, ltd, 1922.

Kenny, Anthony. *Ancient Philosophy - A New History of Western Philosophy, Volume 1*. Oxford University Press, 2006.

Khurana, Varinder. "The Key To Historical Materialism." Nawanzamana (Punjabi), Nov. 2019, p. 4.

Kirilenko, Georgievna Galina, and Lydia Korshunova. *What Is Philosophy?*. Progress Publishers, 1985.

Koyré, Alexandre. "An Unpublished Letter of Robert Hooke to Isaac Newton." *Isis*, vol. 43, no. 4, 1952, pp. 312–37.

Lenin, V. I. *Collected Works Vol. 20*. 3rd ed., Progress Publishers, 1977.

---. "Karl Marx: A Brief Biographical Sketch with an Exposition of Marxism -1914-15." *Lenin Collected Works, Vol. 21*, Progress Publishers, 1974, pp. 43–81.

---. "Lenin's Philosophical Notebooks - 1914-16." *Lenin Collected Works, Vol. 38*, Progress Publishers, 1977.

---. *Materialism and, Empirio-Criticism - 1908*. Progress Publishers, 1977.

---. "On the Significance of Militant Materialism (1922)." Lenin's Collected Works, vol. 33, Progress Publishers, 1972, pp. 227–36.

---. "The Three Sources and Three Component Parts of Marxism - 1913." *Lenin Collected Works, Vol. 19*, Progress Publishers, 1977, pp. 23–28.

Lieberman, Philip. *Eve Spoke: Human Language and Human Evolution*. W.W. Norton and Co., 1998.

---. "On the Nature and Evolution of the Neural Bases of Human Language." *Yearbook of Physical Anthropology*, vol. 45, 2002, pp. 36–62.

---. "Primate Vocalizations and Human Linguistic Ability." *The Journal of the Acoustical Society of America*, vol. 44, no. 6, 1968, pp. 1574–84.

Locke, John. *An Essay Concerning Human Understanding - 1690*. Penguin Classics, 1998.

Luria, Alexander Romanovich. *Traumatic Aphasia*. Humanities Press, 1970.

Lyons, John. *Language and Linguistics (1981)*. Cambridge University Press, 2009.

Madan, Sneh Prabha. "The Origin and Nature of Language." *Reading in Language Studies*, edited by Kshanika Bose and Ramesh C Srivastava, Metropolitan Book Co. (P) Ltd., 1982, pp. 1–22.

Marx, Karl. "Afterword to the Second German Edition - 1873." *Capital A Critique of Political Economy - 1867*, Progress Publishers, 1974.

---. *Capital A Critique of Political Economy - 1867.* Progress Publishers, 1974.

---. "Karl Marx. Theses on Feuerbach - 1845." *Marx and Engels: Collected Works, Vol. 5,* Progress Publishers, 1975, pp. 3–5.

---. "Marx to Ludwig Kugelmann In Hanover, July 11, 1868." *Selected Correspondence of Marx and Engel,* Progress Publishers, 1955, pp. 195–97.

---. "Notes on Epicurean Philosophy - 1839." *Marx and Engels Collected Works, Vol. 1,* International Publishers, 1975, pp. 403–509.

---. "Rheinische Zeitung No. 195, July 14, 1842, Supplement." *Marx and Engels Collected Works, Vol. 1,* International Publishers, 1975, p. 195.

---. "Rheinische Zeitung No. 195, July 14, 1842, Supplement." *Marx and Engels Collected Works, (1835-43),* vol. 1, International Publishers, 1975, pp. 195–202.

Marx, Karl, and Friedrich Engels. *The German Ideology (1846).* Progress Publishers, 1968.

McCrone, John. *The Ape That Spoke: Language and the Evolution of the Human Mind.* William Morrow & Co, 1991.

Müller, Max. "The Theoretical Stage, And The Origin Of Language." *Lectures on the Science of Language: Delivered at the Royal Institution of Great Britain in April, May, & June 1861,* Longmans, Green, 1864, pp. 287–328.

Noiré, Ludwig. *The Origin and Philosophy of Language.* The Open Court Publishing Company, 1917.

Paget, Richard. *Human Speech.* Kegan Paul, Trench, Trübner and Co. Ltd, 1930.

Pavlov, I. P. *I. P. Pavlov, Selected Works.* Edited by S Koshtoyants, Foreign Languages Publishing House, 1955.

Publishers, 1938.

Stross, Brian. *The Origin and Evolution of Language*. Dubuque, Iowa : W. C. Brown Co., 1976.

Thorndike, Edward Lee. "The Origin of Language." *Science*, vol. 98, no. 2531, 1943, pp. 1–6.

Vajda, Edward. J. *The Origin of Language*. http://pandora.cii.wwu.edu/vajda/ling201/test1materials%0A/origin_of_language.htm%0. Accessed 22 Aug. 2018.

Vlasova, T. *Marxist-Leninist Philosophy*. Edited by E Ivanov and Galina Sdobnikova, Progress Publishers, 1987.

Yakhot, O. *What Is Dialectical Materialism?* Progress Publishers, 1965.

Plato. *The Republic of Plato - 380 BCE*. Edited by Allan Bloom, 2nd ed., Basic Books, 1991.

Plato, and Benjamin Jowett. "Cratylus." *The Dialogues of Plato Vol. 1*, Macmillan and Company, 1892, pp. 251–389.

Rawlinson, George. *The History of Herodotus*. The Tandy-Thomas company, 1909.

Rehman, Taimur. *A History of Philosophy: 2 .1 The Milesian School*. Elements Media, 2015, https://youtu.be/u_EPUTp0bvE.

---. *A History of Philosophy 3.3 Heraclitus*. Elements Media, 2015, https://youtu.be/GIyho3u7BpU.

Rousseau, Jean-Jacques. "Essay on the Origin of Languages (1822)." *Essay on the Origin of Languages and Writings Related to Music*, edited by John T. Scott, University Press of New England, 1998, pp. 289–332.

Russell, Bertrand. *A History of Western Philosophy*. George Allen & Unwin Ltd., 1969.

Sankrityayan, Rahul. *Darshan-Digdarshan - 1944*. Kitab Mahal, 2018.

Sapir, Edward. *Language: An Introduction to the Study of Speech*. Harcourt, Brace and Company, 1921.

Saussure, Ferdinand D. *Course in General Linguistics (1916)*. Philosophical Library, 1959.

Self-Pronouncing Edition The Holy Bible: Containing the Old and New Testaments; Translated out of the Original Tongues and with the Former Translations Diligently Compared and Revised; Authorized King James Version. The World Publishing Company, 1945.

Selsam, Howard. *What Is Philosophy?* International Publishers, 1962.

Stalin, J. V. *Dialectical and Historical Materialism*. Progress